Content Marketing Strategies

for Professionals

How to Use Content Marketing and SEO to Communicate with Impact, Generate Sales, and Get Found by Search Engines

Bruce Clay and Murray Newlands

CreateSpace Independent Publishing Platform

North Charleston, South Carolina

ISBN-10: 1494390280

ISBN-13: 978-1494390280

About the Authors

Bruce Clay is founder and president of Bruce Clay, Inc., a global Internet marketing optimization firm providing search engine optimization, pay per click, social media marketing, conversion rate optimization, SEO-friendly web design and architecture, and SEO tools and education. Bruce runs his own SEO training in Southern California, and is regularly a featured trainer at SMX and other Internet marketing events. He is also the co-author of *Search Engine Optimization All-In-One for Dummies*.

For more information, please visit *http://www.bruceclay.com* or follow @BruceClayInc on Twitter.

Murray Newlands is founder and editor of TheMail, a news and information site that covers SEO and tech, as well as mobile, affiliate, email, content, and performance marketing. Murray is also deputy editor of Search Engine Journal, and the author of *Online Marketing: A User's Manual* and *Performance Marketing for Professionals*.

Find more information at *http://www.murraynewlands.com* or connect with Murray on Twitter @MurrayNewlands.

Dedication

I dedicate this book to a wonderful industry, and to my great writing team, without which this book would not have been so expertly prepared. Thank you Virginia, Chelsea and Paula.

– Bruce Clay

To my parents, George and Elizabeth Newlands.

– Murray Newlands

Acknowledgments

The authors gratefully acknowledge those individuals and organizations that contributed to the collective brain trust of this book.

Chelsea Adams	JESS3
Paula Allen	Kristi Kellogg
Jordan Armstrong	Sue Keogh
Blendtec	Virginia Nussey
Michael Brito	Lee Odden
Lisa Buyer	Trent Partridge
Jonathon Colman	Social Media Today
Andy Crestodina	Brian Solis
Alyce Currier	Adam Sutton
Ric Dragon	Wistia

Contents

Chapter 8
Live Events: Where I Get to Tell the Story............................ 143

Chapter 9
Social Media: Talking *with* People, Not at Them 159

Introduction

Wisdom Collected from Many Experts

This book is unique. It blends the perspectives of two authors, both experienced Internet marketers with different specialties. In these pages you'll find practical advice for executing content marketing and SEO *together*. Each chapter presents strategies for creating and simultaneously optimizing a particular type of content to meet your marketing goals.

But that's not all. This book features articles by many experts in the online marketing industry. We invited a number of colleagues to contribute, people who are experimenting and succeeding with their own content marketing strategies. As you read their real-world case studies and stories, we hope you'll pick up ideas you can apply to your own campaigns.

The combined wisdom in this book is meant for CMOs, marketing managers and other professionals tasked with promoting content. We assume you're familiar with Facebook, Twitter and YouTube. Here we'll take you beyond the basics to enable you to become a more effective content marketer.

Chapter 1

Reaching Business Goals with Content Marketing and SEO

What do you consider the most essential ingredient for your business's marketing success?

In today's interactive, multi-channel, full-throttle marketing world, the thing a business cannot do without — its life-sustaining bread — is content. Whether it's website text or in-person appearances, articles or ads, video or audio or pictures, the life of a marketing program depends on a steady supply of nourishing content.

Making sure your content gets noticed is the other essential part. With all the social media, traditional media, and online and offline publishing choices available today, that's a real challenge. Fortunately, getting content found is where search engine optimization comes in.

And it gets really exciting when a strategy aligns content marketing and SEO with revenue goals. Goal-focused, content-producing companies today are watching their KPIs climb.

A New Definition of Content Marketing

So what is content marketing, exactly? Here's our definition:

Content marketing achieves business objectives by strategically creating and sharing content.

Content marketing is not:

- Creating robotic posts stuffed with keywords
- Writing long-winded sales pitches
- Stalking or pestering your customers in social media
- Proliferating content just because you think you have to
- Sharing a diary on your business website of what you ate for lunch
- Scraping content from other websites
- Publishing everywhere your competitors do without considering what is right for your brand

Content marketing is:

- Communicating effectively
- Making connections
- Sharing the right content
- Engaging your audience
- Being in the right place at the right time
- Seizing opportunities
- Inspiring customer action
- Nurturing the needs of your customers
- Showcasing your personality/culture in a way that fits the brand

Why Do Businesses Need Content Marketing?

People have been telling stories since the dawn of time. We are hard-wired to understand information that way. The Internet has leveled the playing field for content creators, allowing anyone the opportunity to create and distribute almost any kind of content. We live in an age of great opportunity where marketers have more power than ever to tell stories through content. But while it's easier than ever to simply publish content, it seems harder than ever to make meaningful content that effectively generates business. More voices mean more clutter, more competition, and a heightened need to strategize, adjust and adapt.

> *The marketer's responsibility is to tell the right story to the right people and organize content around business objectives.*

Connecting with the right people at the right time in the right way with the right message to advance your business goals — that's what content marketing is about. Truly great content marketing communicates effectively, builds community and moves leads closer to being customers. Sharing stories through text, videos, photos, podcasts and memes can be a powerful force to induce sales, retain customers, communicate a brand or even promote a cause. The goal might be to bring customers into a store, rally people to an event or attract visitors to a website. Great online content will achieve these goals through ranking on search engines, drawing links from other websites, stimulating word of mouth and social media attention, and generating inbound traffic.

The saying is true that with great power comes great responsibility. For marketers, that responsibility is to tell the right story to the right people and organize content around business objectives. The challenge is not only to get good content out there, but also to make your "it" the right "it," and to create and share it in a way that cuts through the fluff and makes an impact on your bottom line.

The work of a marketer is to utilize the human needs for connection and story and to communicate messaging that compels people to not only listen, but also buy in and become customers.

Can't I Just Skip the Social Media Party?

A lot of business owners would rather just do business as usual without worrying about Twitter, Facebook, blogs and the like. The problem is that *online is where your customers are*. When you build community online, you're building your customer base and protecting your business reputation. When you don't participate, rest assured competitors will fill in the silence with their own community building. Or worse, negative online comments could take away your customers without your even knowing why.

The smart marketer joins the party, but does it efficiently — with compelling content.

Content has the potential to get people's attention. Developing and sharing useful content for your audience is critical to your bottom line. Plain and simple. In the 21st century, content marketing affects:

- How people perceive your brand
- How many people know you exist
- Whether leads convert to customers
- Whether customers become return customers
- What people say — or don't say—to their friends about you

The Age of Execution

It used to be enough to just be online and publishing content. It meant you were ahead of the curve. Five years ago everyone was talking about the value of starting a blog, sharing content socially and optimizing that content to be found by search engines. These days that's all common practice. If you're not doing those things on some level, you are behind the curve.

The age of experimentation for its own sake is over. It is now the age of execution.

Creating and sharing content for its own sake, or throwing content at a Twitter or Facebook wall to see what sticks, aren't good enough anymore. With so much content being created, the new challenge is to make sure that the content you do create is tied to business objectives, speaks to the right audience and effectively reaches that audience. Any new content approach needs to be developed and tested within the context of objectives, and those objectives defined as specific desired behaviors from a specific target audience.

While it's easier than ever to publish content, it seems harder than ever to make meaningful content that generates business.

Today, all the pieces need each other. As marketers, we've realized by now that social media is less of a shiny new toy and more of an opportunity to do what we've always done, but using the unique advantages of this new channel. And it's the same with every new online content delivery medium. A video that lives online is one incarnation of a moment that happened offline. A blog post is not a separate entity from a live event. There is no need to distinguish between online and offline anymore. They are used together, they enhance each other, and they are all pieces of the same pie.

No matter how it originates or how it is shared, content lives through communication. Good communication tells a compelling story. Great content marketing ties that communication and storytelling to business objectives.

The Role of Search Engine Optimization

Content marketing and search engine optimization (SEO) go together like bread and butter. They complement one another in an inseparable kind of way.

You write content hoping *the right people* will read it at *the right time*; the search engine's job is to find *the right content* and deliver it to *the right people*. You have everything to gain by improving how search engines access, crawl and interpret the content you create. And, conversely, everything to lose by ignoring it.

Search engine optimization is the part of the content marketing equation related to how people find you.

How Technical Is SEO? Do I Have to Learn HTML?

A few years ago, search engine optimization (SEO) was an exciting new innovation. Today it's standard practice and mandatory, not optional, for websites that want to be found through search engines. If you are in the market to be seen and make money online, you need a basic understanding of SEO in order to launch new content successfully.

> *Applying SEO best practices helps make your excellent content worthy of ranking so people can find it through search.*

You don't have to learn HTML to write optimized content. Some SEO elements do involve code though, so you'll want to have someone on your team who can implement necessary SEO changes for your content pages.

For you as a content creator, what's more important than having technical skills is *understanding the principles and best practices* of search engine optimization. Google, Bing, YouTube and the other search engines decide which results are *most relevant* and *most authoritative* for any query. Applying SEO best practices helps make your excellent content worthy of ranking so people can find it through a search engine.

TIP: *For an excellent introduction to SEO, watch Bruce Clay's "Free Executives Guide to SEO" at* http://www.bruceclay.com/seo/free-executive-seo-guide.htm.

How to Save Your Marriage with Content Marketing Strategy

By Chelsea Adams

Step one: Don't tell your wife you want to use content marketing strategy to save your marriage.

Step two: Think long and hard about content marketing best practices and realize that, at the heart of it, **content marketing strategy is all about:**

- Knowing who you are as an individual or a brand and then, presenting the best possible "you" to the world (*not the scatterbrained you that doesn't think before speaking*).

- Listening and taking the time to really understand who it is you're talking to, how they prefer to be spoken to, and what they're interested in.

- Communicating in a focused, intentional way that helps solve problems— or entertain, or inform, or philosophize, or . . .

- Being yourself! Sharing your personality, connecting with like-minded people, and making a lasting impression.

- Curating or otherwise sharing the ideas/tips/resources that inspire you and/or represent your brand. Or—put another way—*not talking about yourself all the time.*

- Trying new things.

- Going where the conversation is. For instance, if the people you want to talk to are always on Instagram and never on Twitter, why are you on Twitter and not Instagram?

- Behaving ethically. *Don't steal anyone's content, or promote your blog with links purchased with the intention of boosting search rankings.*

- Setting goals. *How will you know you succeed if you haven't set a goal?*

- Keeping track of your efforts, observing the results, and reflecting on your observations to determine what's working and what's failing miserably.

- Learning from your mistakes and doing more of what works and less of what doesn't!

Step three: Re-read the points outlined in Step Two and realize that — *ta da!* — you can apply every one of those steps to your relationship with your wife (or whichever relationship you're wanting to improve).

Step four: Take a moment to consider how much better our relationships would be if we all tried to figure ourselves out before we tried to figure anyone else out; listened;

How to Save Your Marriage with Content Marketing Strategy
(continued)

thought about who we were speaking to before speaking; communicated in ways that reflect forethought and consideration for listeners; behaved ethically; were actively self-reflective; observed the cause and effect that our participation in the world inspires; and actually learned from our observations.

Step five: Forgive yourself for perhaps having approached both your content marketing strategy and your marriage from the wrong direction. Then, consider reassessing the default way you've fostered and nurtured (or not fostered/nurtured) both.

Step six: Realize how completely human content marketing is, and that every aspect of it needs to be approached with a "by humans, for humans" mentality.

Step seven: After your marriage is fixed, tell your wife you used content marketing strategy to make yourself a better communicator. She'll probably laugh—either because she's also in the industry or because you're a huge nerd and that's why she married you.

Step eight: After you've fixed your content marketing, tell your social media communities and your blog readers how you did it! Maybe even share with them how you applied content marketing strategy to save your marriage. The story will show your personality, teach your community a lesson, and—at the very least—make a lasting impression.

Chelsea Adams is a Bruce Clay, Inc. senior content writer interested in SEO, cob building, and energized language that motivates. Follow her on Twitter @ChelseaBeaAdams.

Chapter 2

Planning a Content Marketing Campaign

Content marketing is about hitting business and marketing objectives through creating and sharing the right content. Anyone who tells you otherwise will not be in a job for long.

In this chapter you'll find out why most companies' content marketing approach is backward. Through a three-phase strategy, we'll lay out practical ways you can avoid this trap and instead establish objectives, target the right audience and choose your content effectively.

The Wrong Approach

All too often marketing campaigns get started in the wrong order.

Imagine the scene. Someone on your team reads about a new social media platform and opens an account, starts connecting with people, and shares some content. As they get used to the network, they start to figure out who the most active people are. And then, a few weeks later, the team meets to talk about what the company could try to do with this new account and these new connections. Soon the meeting becomes a brainstorming session about what everyone thinks could be done with this new network presence. Action items include looking into it and reporting back at the next meeting.

We've all been at those meetings. Maybe you were at one this morning.

It's backward. That model looks like this:

1. Content
2. Audience
3. Objectives

Is There a Better Way?

Content creation is a part of your marketing strategy and as such, should be approached *strategically*. Does it make any sense to execute before you have a clear idea of what you want to accomplish? Before there are established objectives and the research to support them?

It's absolutely essential to figure out who you're talking with and why before you start yammering.

The time of throwing content at the wall to see what sticks is over. We're not discovering the Internet, blogs, social media, apps and all the rest anymore. Whatever content you're creating for whatever platform, you shouldn't bring it into existence for its own sake. Creating videos because your office got a new camera isn't content marketing. Using Pinterest because it's new isn't good content marketing.

In order for communication to be effective, you have to know who you want to communicate with and how your whole team defines "effective." For instance, would you call your content effective because a person buys a product? Stays on the site for a certain amount of time? Reads more content? Likes you on Facebook?

Every business model will have different goals. It's impossible to know whether your content strategy is meeting these goals if no one has decided what the goals are.

That said, a successful content marketing strategy flips the ineffective Content-Audience-Objectives model outlined above upside down. It emphasizes figuring out what you want to accomplish and whom you want to communicate with first, before any effort is spent creating content.

The new model reorders the content marketing process, like this:

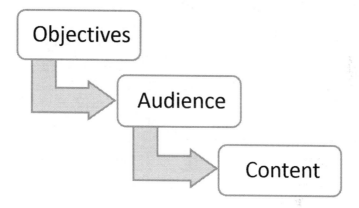

That's right. The "Content" in a successful content marketing campaign comes *third*.

To see success, it's absolutely essential to figure out who you're talking with and why before you start yammering. Remember, we're not creating content just for the sake of creating content anymore. It's crucial that all efforts be rooted in purpose and driven by the needs of your target audience.

What Makes Content Marketing New

The tactics of content marketing bring together many disciplines to tell the right story through online and offline content. It pulls from lessons learned in advertising, sales, traditional marketing, social media, branding, event planning and more, then reframes the purpose of all of the content a business creates. Content marketing shatters the silos that divide the various departments, which can confuse the message, and creates a strategic framework for cohesively telling the company's story.

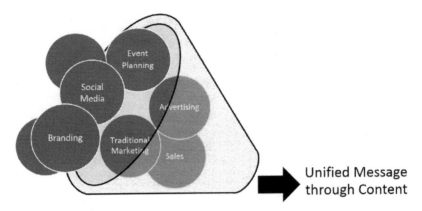

Unified Message through Content

Figure 2-1: Content marketing has a funnel effect that unifies your brand message.

The power of content marketing is that it pulls techniques from many different specialties into the same funnel, morphs them into a compelling story, and creates a more unified message that is a powerful marketing force.

Laying a Foundation for a Content Marketing Campaign

Let's get practical. Now that you understand *what* to do first, second and third when planning a content marketing campaign, *how* should you do it? Read on. For the rest of this chapter, we'll cover the how-to in three phases: objectives, audience and content.

Phase One: Establishing Objectives

Since objectives are the basic driving force for everything you do in content marketing, begin by considering questions like these:

- Why are you creating content?
- What do you want to happen as a result?
- What metrics can you reference to determine if your

content strategy is effective?

Here are some typical high-level business objectives that could benefit from a content marketing campaign:

- Sell more of something
- Acquire new customers
- Build customer loyalty
- Get your current customers to buy more of something
- Get more people to a given landing page
- Get more exposure
- Give something away
- Get more readers
- Strengthen your brand image

Brainstorming high-level objectives like the ones listed above is a good place to start. Simply ask yourself, *what do I want to accomplish?* Then jot down some responses.

Once you understand the high-level objectives, it's important to define success by making your objectives specific, measurable and time-bound. The more explicit you can be with your objectives, the better.

For example, once you identify that you want to "sell more," next work on making your objective

Your target audience needs to be aware of your stories and content long before you want them to buy from you.

specific and time-bound. If you don't, Bob might think the goal is to sell 10 more memberships in a year, while Julie thinks it's to sell 1,000 memberships in three months.

A measurable objective such as "sell 250 monthly memberships in Q1 of 2014" or "sell 800 annual memberships between January 1 and June 30" gets everyone on the same page. It clearly defines the target and allows your team to determine if they are on track to meet or exceed the goal. A specific measurable objective also lets you monitor progress and make strategic adjustments as needed.

Because every industry and every company has different demands, there are no one-size-fits-all objectives. Be introspective and really consider the needs of your company. Use your analytics data, user-behavior research and other statistics to inform your objective metrics. It's okay to have ambitious objectives, but you want to make sure your goals are research-based and attainable; there's nothing strategic about pulling numbers out of thin air and setting yourself up for failure.

Make Relationship Building One of My Goals

In today's service-oriented marketplace, almost every organization should make building customer relationships a top objective. Much of the power of content marketing comes through creating relationships with potential and current customers and clients.

The longer the relationship, the more established you are in their minds and the more likely they are to buy from you. Stores boast of being "Established in 1859," and consultants talk about having "20 years of experience" to show that they are trustworthy. That kind of credibility is powerful.

Content marketing has the power to create that kind of history of experience and credibility with customers even faster, by acting out that relationship in real time. The longer the relationship, the more established you become in their minds and the more likely they are to buy from you. And referrals from trusted friends, such as people can so easily find on social media platforms, strengthens or builds a foundation for those trust relationships.

Knowing who reads your blogs, watches your videos, and buys your products gives you valuable marketing intelligence.

We know that people take action much more quickly based on direct word of mouth or social media recommendations from trusted sources. We also know, from advertising, that people need to see an ad x number of times before acting on it. Think of content marketing as combining both of those approaches and providing repeated exposure to valuable content that's part of a larger brand story. When it's your brand telling that story and building relationships in the process, customers develop familiarity and trust. They become more likely to take action when you have the right product and offer.

Because of the nature of relationships and storytelling, content marketing cannot be a turn on/off type of thing. You can't wait until you're ready to make sales to start doing it. If you want to build up trust to acquire and retain customers, you have to establish a brand reputation over time.

Never before have marketers had so much customer information at their fingertips. On the flip side, through content marketing you can enable people to get to know your organization, too. Your target audience needs to be aware of your stories and content long before you want them to buy from you. Then when it's time for that purchase decision, they'll have more reason to choose you.

Phase Two: Identifying My Audience

Once you understand the business objectives you want to pursue, next you'll determine the audience you need to communicate with to fulfill those objectives. You need to figure out whom you're already talking to, what types of people you need to be talking to, and how you can get closer to meeting your objectives by addressing those people effectively.

All kinds of people go searching for content for all kinds of reasons. What kinds of people come looking for yours? Knowing *who* the people are that read your blogs, watch your videos, and buy your products gives you valuable marketing intelligence. Knowing *when* they consume your content and *why* can help you figure out how to create content that better serves their needs.

But what if you don't have current customer data to analyze? Even when you launch a new business or product line, identify the audience you want to reach. Otherwise, you'll try to appeal to everyone — and make bland content that won't interest anyone.

We've laid out four steps below that will help you determine your audience and begin to strategize how to reach them.

1) Do In-House Research

You can perform persona research as in-depth as your budget and schedule permits. A business could spend tens of thousands of dollars talking one-on-one with actual consumers and doing thorough market research. But if you're working with a low or non-existent budget, start with what you already have.

Spend time talking with your customer service and sales people to get insight into your existing market base. Consider asking your internal staff for information like:

- What questions do people ask when they call in?
- What do they like/not like about our service and products?
- What are they interested in knowing more about?
- Do you see any patterns in the types of people who ask about that?

Statements like, "Mostly women inquire about XYZ" should catch your attention. Those are valuable tidbits for persona research.

2) Do Market Research Online

Beyond looking at customer data, you can take your market research and segmentation a long way just by using free web resources.

The wealth of statistics available online are especially helpful if you have a local or regional market area to focus on. Using sites like the **US Census Bureau** (*www.census.gov*), **Zillow** (*www.zillow.com*), **City-Data** (*www.city-data.com*) and others that compile demographics data, you can discover detailed facts about populations (see example in Figure 2-2). With this data you can begin to segment your audience.

Learn as much as you can about your target audiences — their interests, values, shopping habits, hobbies, etc. Get as much detail as possible so you can identify who your "ideal" customers are.

pinterest

House

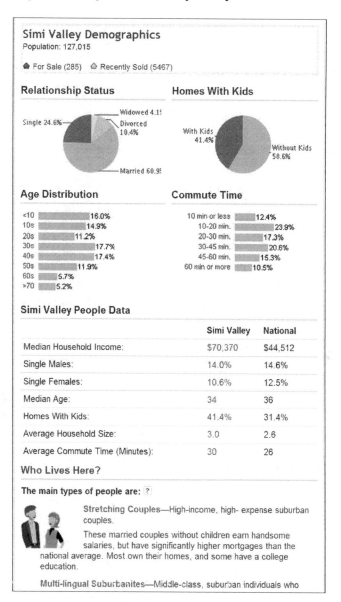

Figure 2-2: Research can include free online data such as this page from Zillow.com.

3) Learn Where Personas Spend Time Online

Where are the people you want to talk to? Are they on your website already or do you need to lure them in? Discovering where your personas spend time online is the next step in persona research.

Find out what blogs they read, what forums they participate in, what media they watch, and where they "hang out" online. Some of this information you can glean from analytics reports, if people that fit the geographical qualifications of your target persona are currently interacting with your blog content or your website. You can find this information in **Google Analytics** (especially the Demographics Reports) or another reporting tool.

Other methods of learning about your customer groups include using customer surveys, one-on-one interviews, and even reaching out to connect with individual customers on Facebook, Twitter or other sites online. While more labor-intensive, this kind of research can develop stronger customer relationships and give you highly reliable data for your persona research.

As you follow your persona groups to their favorite web locations, you'll make lots of valuable discoveries you can apply to your own content marketing strategy. Here are some things you can learn:

- The kinds of content they like to consume (video, audio, games, humor, quick tips, images, long-form essays, etc.)
- Appropriate voice, style and personality
- Their interests and what they like to talk about
- Words they use to refer to your subject area
- How they spend their free time and work time
- How they do research and make purchase decisions
- Social networks they use (which tells you more about how they prefer to receive communication)
- How frequently they use the Internet (for fun and work)
- What platform do they use more, mobile or desktop?

4) Create Persona Profiles

Now gather all the audience data you've accumulated. It's time to turn it into something your whole content team can grab hold of.

Big picture, you want to categorize the people who will read your content into need- or interest-based groups, each represented by a persona. Persona groups help you associate names, faces, interests and desires with the different segments of your audience or market. Then create a profile for each persona (see Figure 2-3).

You might be surprised what a difference it makes to write to an actual embodiment of a person, someone with a name, face and real needs, rather than to a vague "anyone." In everyday conversation, you change your words and give more or less detail depending on who's listening. For content online, your message also should change for different audiences. You would use different words and stress different product benefits depending on whom you're talking to. Having a persona in mind helps you make content that serves and appeals to a particular audience group.

It is not uncommon for persona research reports to include:

- **Descriptive Title:** Give each need-derived persona group a name or title that describes those people. For example, if you own a company that sells cars, your persona groups might be "Off-Road Weekend Warrior," "Family Person Concerned with Capacity and Safety," "Businessman with Expendable Income," and "Fashion-Focused Car Lessee."

- **Demographic Profile:** Information about the collective behavior of individuals that fall into this category might include age, personality characteristics, interests, goals and behaviors.

- **Personal Identifiers:** A fictitious photo (i.e., avatar), name and biography of one person that represents the collective persona can be useful. This bio may tell about the persona's income, job, family and other circumstances.

- **Slogan:** Find a quote from the research that summarizes the persona in a nutshell. For instance, "Having a car that can fit a little league team is important to me."

Paul - "The Lifelong Learner"

"The industry is always changing and evolving, so I need to be changing and evolving all the time, too"

About Paul:

Paul is an accomplished online marketer, but he never feels "done." Paul is interested in staying on top of the latest industry changes and trends — from technology shifts, to changes in strategic thinking. He hates saying "I don't know" and gets personal satisfaction from learning new things.

He will spend hours online reading tech news or taking self-guided training. He is primarily interested in learning new skills that will help make him a stronger online marketer.

Age: 33
Status: Married
Title: In-House Marketing Manager
Mobile user - iPhone

Motivations:
- Recognizes the industry is always changing and that he needs to adapt to stay afloat
- Wants to stay a step ahead of his competition
- Gets a feeling of personal accomplishment when he learns something new

Pain Points:
- Doesn't have a lot of time
- Retains information better with video than written word
- Dislikes streaming; wants to be able to download video and watch whenever

Figure 2-3: Your fictitious persona profiles can be fleshed out with personal details.

Though home life and personal circumstances may seem like arbitrary information, what personas really provide is a 360-degree perspective on what these types of people's lives are like, what they care about, and how you can best serve them when they need you the most. To better visualize and relate to personas, many marketers create contact cards such as the one shown above (see Figure 2-3). Imagine handing a card like this to one of your copywriters. The card would make it a lot easier for the copywriter to create content that speaks to this audience segment and directly meets their needs.

Make your persona research a living document, as this list will certainly change over the lifespan of your content marketing.

CASE STUDY
Content Marketing: Targeted Persona Strategy Lifts Sales Leads 124%

By Adam Sutton

Content quality is in the eye of the beholder. You have to understand the audience before you can "wow" it with great blog posts, white papers and webinars.

The marketing team at Skytap, a self-service provider of cloud automation solutions, understands this well.

"In the last 12 to 18 months, we have put a lot of focus and energy toward understanding who our buyers and personas are in any given deal, and then catering our content to those groups," says Nate Odell, director of marketing for Skytap.

Skytap launched a content marketing strategy in May 2012 to generate and convert more leads. The team saw great year-over-year results:

- 210% increase in North American site traffic
- 55% increase in organic search traffic
- 97% increase in leads from online marketing
- 124% increase in leads from all channels (online as well as offline events and programs)
- 73% increase in opportunities from online marketing

"If we didn't have content, I don't believe that we would have had as much success as we did in 2012," Odell says. "Content marketing is just so crucial."

The team's strategy is founded on a deep understanding of its prospects and buyers. Here's how the team set that foundation and improved upon it:

Step #1. Set basic audience segments
Skytap's customers are typically middle- and enterprise-level companies who use cloud computing to accomplish three specific tasks. These "use-cases," as Odell calls them, give Skytap a natural way to segment its content marketing strategy.

Step #2. Research the segments
Skytap wanted to target its content to key players within these groups to give it more impact. The team collected research from many sources, including CRM and lead-tracking data, search and other behavioral data, information from sales reps, and conversations with existing customers.

Step #3. Dig deeper in each segment
In its research, the team wanted to identify the typical roles involved in a sales deal for each of Skytap's three use-cases. The business titles typically involved in the deals were important pieces of information. For example, this could be a senior software

CASE STUDY – Content Marketing: Targeted Persona Strategy Lifts Sales Leads 124% (continued)

engineer who is asked to evaluate a solution as part of the sales process.

"It's really important for us to find patterns around the titles we see in deals in each use-case so we can know with probably 90-95% accuracy that if we approach these folks in other organizations who are similar, we are going to have a much higher rate of success selling into these organizations," says Odell.

Create a profile: The team examines the common characteristics of people in these roles to create a full persona. This includes gathering information about each persona:

- Product of interest (use-case)
- How they found relevant information
- What they searched for online
- Relevant pain points
- Obstacles that prevent the person from moving forward

Start with important roles: Creating this many personas is a big task. Odell is careful not to let the project spiral out of control: "Instead of saying, 'Let's just go understand everybody,' we need to be very methodical and say, 'Let's go understand the particular use-cases and all the individuals we typically see in those deals and really understand what they're looking for.'"

Step #4. Plan targeted content
Since targeted marketing typically earns a better response than generic marketing, Skytap strives to target particular use-cases and personas in its content.

Step #5. Establish a content review process
Skytap publishes a steady stream of high-quality content. Since its audience is highly specialized, and the topics are very granular, the company has a rigorous review process and a managing editor to ensure the material meets a high bar.

Adam Sutton is a senior reporter with MarketingSherpa, a research firm specializing in tracking what works in all aspects of marketing. This article is excerpted from the original case study published at *http://www.marketingsherpa.com/article/case-study/targeted-persona-content-marketing-strategy*.

Phase Three: Auditing and Creating Content

Once you've established the objective and have your audience in mind, you're ready to start strategizing content.

Looking Around: What Content is Currently Working?

Your first step should be to survey what content you already have out there and what effect, positive or negative, it is having at the moment. This is often called a *content audit* and can be as in depth or cursory as you like. If you have the time and resources, by all means, dig deep. If you're strapped for time and money, you can still get a general idea and pull some relevant or prominent content samples.

> *The key is to choose the outlet and content that will reach the right people and tie back to your business objectives.*

When doing a content audit, remember to evaluate your current content on several levels. Look at how popular the content is — did people like it, share it, etc. — and whether its popularity continued over time. How much traffic did it bring to your website, and how many conversions? Is it helping you achieve your specific monthly, quarterly and annual objectives? If a piece of content is achieving objectives, try to identify which persona the content is resonating with. This will help give you a better idea of who your healthiest personas are and, accordingly, which of your personas are not as active and may need more attention. Make a note to create more content similar to your current content that is performing well.

If you find that some of your content is not related to any of your personas but is nonetheless successful, you may have uncovered a new persona that you have previously overlooked.

Prove the Value of Your Content with an Audit

By Jonathon Colman

Think you know your content? OK, how many pages do you have and where are they located? What's the condition of your code and media files? Does your content contain all of the metadata it needs? When was it last updated? How is it performing with your target audiences? Does it load quickly? And who in the organization manages it?

More importantly: is the content any good? Does it meet the needs of your customers or users? Does it inspire confidence and loyalty? Is it trustworthy? Is it share-worthy?

That's the value provided by a content audit—it helps you answer questions about quality and performance. Ultimately, a good audit helps you classify your content into four levels of quality:

- **Gold:** Content your audience loves that represents the brand well
- **Silver:** Content your audience loves that isn't pulling its weight for the brand
- **Bronze:** Content the brand loves, but that doesn't connect with your audience
- **Tin foil:** Content that everyone hates, or that they simply can't find or use

Here's a secret: you probably have more silver content than gold, more bronze than silver, and way more tin foil than you'd ever expect. But you won't know any of that—or be able to improve the state of content experiences across your site—without going over every single page.

Let's get started with your content audit:

1. Crawl your site and generate a complete inventory of all of its contents. (TIP: Use the Content Analysis Tool at *http://www.content-insight.com* or Screaming Frog at *http://www.screamingfrog.co.uk.*)

2. Export the inventory data to Excel, and then add data from Google Analytics using Excellent Analytics (*http://excellentanalytics.com*). For each URL, metrics like visits, conversion rate, bounce rate, page load time, and other quantitative metrics can help you determine how your content is connecting (or not connecting) with your audiences.

3. Then use SEOGadget for Excel (*http://seogadget.com/tools/seogadget-for-excel*) to draw in data about each URL: links, social sharing information, and more. This helps you understand the overall visibility and competitive reach of your content as well as whether or not it's good enough for visitors to share.

4. Now that you have your quantitative data in place, it's time for the really hard work: making honest, qualitative judgments about your content. Go through each

Prove the Value of Your Content with an Audit (continued)

of your pages and examine them against your brand. Do they live up to your brand tenets and core values? Are they simple enough for your target audiences to use and understand? Do they inspire trust and build community? Do they meet the spirit of your voice and tone?

PRO TIP: Have too much content to review manually? You can create a sampling strategy: review pages that are representative of a particular page type or template in cases where much of the content and interface is the same across hundreds or thousands of pages. This saves you time while helping you focus on the biggest wins.

5. Use the "Forrester Web Site User Experience Review" (*http://blogs.forrester.com/adele_sage/10-01-13-announcing_forresters_web_site_user_experience_review_version_8*) to rate the quality of each page on your site against 25 of the most common user experience heuristics. This can help you catch simple problems and make you aware of trending issues across your site.

6. Finally, draw your line in the sand by making a formal recommendation for each piece of content: "Keep," "Change" or "Kill." This saves you from ruining what's already working, helps you optimize the content that's worth saving, and lets you trash everything else. It's not a sin to remove content from your site, especially when it isn't working for your audience or your brand. You're better off without it!

While content audits support your testing and content marketing strategies, remember that audits are just one step along the road to content strategy. At some point, you'll need to stop auditing and start acting on your findings. Keep a running log of opportunities as you audit your pages so that you can prioritize them for action. Measure (and communicate!) the results of your work as you go so that you can stay focused on the optimizations that have the greatest long-term impact.

Working from the quantitative and qualitative data in your audit, there's nothing that you can't accomplish for your brand and audiences. Happy auditing!

For over 15 years, Jonathon Colman has helped people and organizations build, find, and use the best stuff on the web. Jonathon is a content strategist at Facebook, a Webby Award winner, and a coffee snob. You can learn more about him at jonathoncolman.org or contact him on Twitter @jcolman.

Creating New Content: How Can I Reach Them?

Once you know what you want to have happen (your objectives) and who you need to talk to (your audience), it's time to start creating and sharing content.

Knowing that you want to design your content marketing around business objectives with specific indicators of success, how do you decide what kinds of content you should create? Should you *curate content* (i.e., find relevant content from other sources and share it) or write original articles? Should you make videos, run a contest, post funny memes, all of the above? Or should you do something completely different?

There are so many different ways to create and share content that it's easy for it to get overwhelming well before it starts getting helpful. The key is to choose the outlet and the content that will reach the right people and tie back to your business objectives.

Keep in mind that different types of content will help you meet different objectives. Some types of content may help you reach several objectives all at once.

- **Text**, for example, is comparatively easy and fast to produce and can be shared easily on networks like Twitter and LinkedIn.

- **Photos** share well on Facebook, Instagram, Pinterest and others.

- **Videos** do not share as well as images do on social networks, but they have a deeper level of customer engagement.

Remember, your different personas like to consume information in different ways, so your content marketing plan should contain a variety of elements.

What's being said? It can be helpful to survey the current landscape of conversations happening around your topic and your competitors. What are people buzzing about right now? Try to glean how involvement in these conversations could positively affect your business. Remember to keep who you consider to be your "competitors" relatively broad. Companies are often surprised by who their competition is and what conversations they could benefit from. Learn from what is working for your competitors.

What's happening? Don't forget to capitalize on local events as content catalysts, as well. For instance, if you are a local gas station, what kind of content will get event visitors from out of town to come buy gas at your station rather than your competitors'? If the local film festival, muscle car show or parade happens next month, how can you create content that capitalizes on this event?

We're Just Getting Started

Consider this section an introduction to get you started creating a sustainable content strategy. The rest of this book takes you in depth looking at different types of content. You'll discover how to approach them as part of an overall marketing program including how to build on what's working and how to use SEO, keyword research, PPC ads and social media as driving forces in your content strategy.

Chapter 3

Choosing Content Topics that Lead to Customers

Making the right content to engage your audience is critical to the success of any content marketing campaign. In this chapter we'll explore a key question that you must answer:

What should I make content about?

Build on What's Working

In business we often approach strategy by identifying a problem and solving it. This helps us fill holes. However, when you start out with content marketing, it's important to build on what you're doing already that is working.

Once you have done some level of a content audit, you'll have a clear picture of what kind of content you have out there, what campaigns you've already tried or are currently doing that have impact, and a sense of what kind of content you are already good at creating and putting out there.

What Types of Content Work Best

Reviewing your content analytics should tell you what content is generating traffic, leads, sales or other success metrics. If your goals can be measured by website activity, dig into your Google Analytics reports for the information; if not, then look at whatever will tell you how well an initiative worked. Once you identify what content has done well, you can make your next wave of content marketing out of additional content that targets what is already successful.

Organizing your whole website according to themes is one of the best ways to increase your site's ability to rank for your main subjects. This technique is called siloing.

Content analytics can offer incredible insight. From character counts to reading level to subject matter, knowing what your readers like and don't like can help you focus your time on creating more of the stuff that engages and results in conversion, and less of your time on the stuff that doesn't.

For instance, if your content audit shows that 50 percent of your conversions happen on 500-word articles and only 7 percent on 2,500-word articles, you can safely conclude that your short articles engage your demographic better than long ones do. So, based on this audit, it would be wise for your writing team to limit their article length whenever possible.

People are more apt to make purchases if they feel satisfied. Taking the time to research what specific types of content satisfy the needs of your target market pays off, encouraging word of mouth marketing, social sharing, engagement, longer visits and product purchases. It's also valuable to understand what makes content unsatisfying — too long or short, confusing, hard to find or otherwise disenchanting — so you can avoid missed opportunities.

What Topics Work Best

Look at the topics of your most successful content articles, videos, posts, etc. What are they about? What subjects have generated the most audience interest and met your goals?

Building additional content based on winning topics you identify in your audit can have significant user experience and SEO benefits. From a user's perspective, a website with many pages of in-depth coverage on a subject looks like a reliable, even expert, source. There's a higher chance users will find what they're looking for and feel more satisfied with the experience. On the other hand, users will probably bounce right out of a website where the content seems thin, weak or disorganized.

Not surprisingly, search engines look for *content clusters* on one particular topic in order to evaluate a website's relevance to a search query. Sites with well-organized structures and many pages focused on single subjects tend to rank higher in search results pages (SERPs). In fact, organizing your whole website according to themes is one of the best ways to increase your site's ability to rank for your main subjects and terms. This site-architecture technique is called *siloing*. To do it, begin with your main navigation elements as the primary "silos" of information, and then clearly group theme-related pages together by linking them strategically within their silos.

If you know you have content that draws a lot of traffic for one topic or term, create more content around that topic. Doing so will reinforce your relevance and strengthen your search ranking for that topic, which can lead to more traffic.

TIP: *BruceClay.com has many articles on how to silo a website for maximum SEO benefit. We recommend you start with the "SEO Siloing" article and explore from there:* http://www.bruceclay.com/seo/silo.htm

Strategizing a New Campaign

Creating a content marketing campaign around a handful of keywords that are relevant to your target audience is a savvy way to kick off a new campaign. It's important to make sure that the keywords you select and the content you create fits firmly within your overall and long-term branding and brand story, but when it comes to tactical maneuvering, it's hard to beat a solid keyword strategy.

Search engines look for words and phrases repeated naturally within content, also known as *keywords*, in order to understand what a web page is about. If you're writing a new page of content, choose a single subject to focus on and make that topic clear by using relevant keywords, some word-stemmed variations of those keywords (e.g., *write, writer, writing*) and also related wording in a way that reads naturally throughout the text.

What marketers do not like having some hard analytics to back up their decisions? Knowing what keywords and topics will drive traffic and generate leads can be the starting point for building the next chapter of your brand story. This kind of an approach begins with research.

1) Keyword Research Tools

Search engine keyword tools have long supported targeting for content marketing campaigns:

- **Google AdWords Keyword Planner** (*http://www.googlekeywordtool.com/*): This favorite tool tells you how many people search for a particular keyword in Google every month and suggests other related phrases searchers use (see Figure 3-1).

- **YouTube Keyword Tool** (*https://www.youtube.com/keyword_tool*): This is an essential resource if you are planning a video content campaign or want to include video as an arm of your campaign.

- **Bing Keyword Research Tool** (*http://www.bing.com/toolbox/keywords*): This user-friendly keyword research tool presents information based on Bing's organic search data.

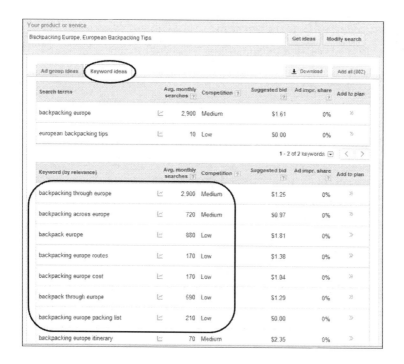

Figure 3-1: Google's Keyword Planner generates keyword ideas along with how frequently they are searched and how competitive they are.

Many third-party sites also offer robust keyword research tools that can expose useful phrases to write content around. You can pay for a subscription-based service and get more bells and whistles, but there are lots of free tools on the web for doing keyword research. Try these:

- **Bruce Clay, Inc.** (*http://www.bruceclay.com/seo/search-engine-optimization.htm*): Embedded in this SEO tutorial are free versions of many of the company's subscription-based SEOToolSet® tools. (Disclaimer: This is author Bruce Clay's company.)

- **Wordtracker** (*http://www.wordtracker.com*): Finds keywords related to your search term.

- **Keyword Eye** (*http://keywordeye.com*): Gives you a unique, visual "keyword cloud" to help you brainstorm keywords.

- **Alexa** (*http://www.alexa.com*): An Amazon property, Alexa analyzes web metrics to show you the top keywords and other interesting facts about your website as well as some top sites by keyword.

- **UberSuggest** (*http://ubersuggest.org*): Pulling from Google Suggest and other sources, this tool shows extensive lists of keyword suggestions in your choice of language and search channel (web, news, images, shopping, etc.).

- **WordStream** (*http://www.wordstream.com/keywords*): Provides a limited number of free searches for keyword suggestions.

TIP: For more on performing keyword research and using tools strategically, go to http://www.bruceclay.com/keyword-research.htm.

2) Suggested Search

Targeting specific, longer keyword phrases on your web pages (known as "long-tail" keywords) can bring you people who are already sure of what they want, rather than people just starting their pre-buying research and searching for more general keywords. To find relevant long-tail keywords, the suggested search box may well be your answer.

Search engines like Google now commonly offer suggested search terms as you type, displaying below the search box as shown here:

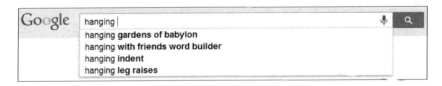

Figure 3-2: Search engine suggestions reveal commonly searched phrases as you type.

To try it out quickly for yourself, pop over to Google.com and start typing something you might create content about for your company. You'll see a dropdown list of different suggested keyword phrases based on what you typed. Every potential customer or lead out there is seeing those same long-tail keyword suggestions. It makes sense to craft some content around these commonly searched phrases.

3) Competitors

Looking at your competitors' websites can give you another great source of content topic ideas — not to copy from, but to stimulate keyword or content ideas that you know you could do even better.

Look at Competitors' Meta Tags

Your competitors' Meta tags can tell you about what they think is important. Search engines still put a lot of emphasis on these tags that are written into the HTML code of most web pages. The Title and Meta Description tags, in particular, usually show up in the SERPs as the big blue link and the black description text. So they influence not only your search engine rankings but also whether users will like what they see enough to click through to your site.

Because these tags carry so much SEO weight, reviewing Meta tags can be a great place to start figuring out your competitors' keyword targets. You'll get a behind-the-scenes look at what keyword traffic they are trying to attract. Remember that this research is only as good as the competitors are, and you may see a wide variety of terms. Not everything you find will be actionable, but understanding their campaigns will help you sharpen yours.

How to Review Meta Tags

You can see a web page's Meta tags in two ways.

- **View as HTML:** With the web page open, look at the HTML code directly by pressing *Ctrl+U* or choosing View Source from the browser menu. The tags should be located in the head section at the top.

- **Use a tool:** If you're not comfortable reading HTML code,

take advantage of tools that extract the critical SEO
information and give it to you in an easy-to-read format.
There are many tools that do this one page at a time. But if
you want to view several competing pages' tags all at once
so you can compare them, try Bruce Clay, Inc.'s free **SEO
Multi-Page Information Tool**
(*http://www.bruceclay.com/seo/search-engine-
optimization.htm*), as shown in Figure 3-3.

http://www.ebay.com/gds/How-to-Measure-Your-Finger-for-Your-Ring-Size-/10000000000067477/g.html	
Tag	Content
Title	How to Measure Your Finger for Your Ring Size	eBay
Description	The most important factor when purchasing any ring, is making sure it fits eLuxé Jewelry provides you with the most comprehensive way. (maybe the only way) to measure your finger. 1. Wrap a piece of string...
Keywords	ring gemstone diamond engagement anniversary
H1	How to Measure Your Finger for Your Ring Size
Canonical	http://www.ebay.com/gds/How-to-Measure-Your-Finger-for-Your-Ring-Size-/10000000000067477/g.html

http://www.wikihow.com/Find-Your-Ring-Size	
Tag	Content
Title	How to Find Your Ring Size (with Printable Ring Sizer) - wikiHow
Description	How to Find Your Ring Size. While the most precise way to find your ring size is to have a jeweler do it, you can easily do it at home. Whether you're sizing your finger to buy a ring online, or want to surprise your sweetie with an...
Keywords	WikiHow, Find Your Ring Size, wiki, how to articles, how to instructions, DIY, tips, howto, learn, how do I
H1	How to Find Your Ring Size
Canonical	http://www.wikihow.com/Find-Your-Ring-Size

http://findmyringsize.com/	
Tag	Content
Title	Ring Size Chart - determine your ring size using online ring sizer
Description	Find your ring size online! Use FindMyRingSize.com to measure your ring size instantly. No need for printing, or waiting for mail delivered ring sizer.

Figure 3-3: *Using an SEO tool such as this free report on BruceClay.com, you can review the Meta tags of up to 6 URLs at once.*

Dig for Competitors' Keywords

Competitive research tools such as **Compete**
(*http://www.compete.com*), **Alexa** (*http://www.alexa.com*) and
Keyword Spy (*http://www.keywordspy.com*) can tell you the
search terms that bring traffic to your competitors' sites. Some of
these terms will be relevant to your marketing and some irrelevant.
But sift through them to find new topics of inspiration.

Looking at a competitor's *backlinks*, the clickable text used in links
that point to the competitor's site, also reveals competitor

keywords. Backlink competitive tools such as **Linkdex** (*http://www.linkdex.com*) provide not only the terms being used to link to your competitors' sites, but also the external sites where those links reside. Researching all of those may spark valuable topic and content-improvement ideas that your competitors are missing.

4) PPC Ads

Pay-per-click (PPC) ads in search engines offer marketers a versatile testing ground for keyword and content ideas. PPC advertising can be set up quickly and often for less money than creating a content campaign. PPC is particularly useful if you are starting a new project.

> *The knowledge you gain from a small investment in pay-per-click . . . may save you tens of thousands of dollars.*

Advertising is not only a good way to drive leads, it can be a powerful tool to research what kind of keywords and phrases your customers are looking for. Use PPC advertising to find terms that convert customers and then create content campaigns to target those terms. (See Chapter 10 for more on PPC.)

Run PPC Ads as Research

If you invest, say, $1,000 running a PPC campaign for a month around 5 to 10 different terms related to your business, you will end the month with a clearer picture of what your potential customers will click on to get to your site. For example, if you have a dog grooming business and you run pay-per-click ads through Google, Bing and Facebook around terms like "Dog Grooming," "Get my dog a bath" and several others like it, you may find that one or two terms get more clicks than the rest.

If PPC tests show the most effective term is "Dog Grooming," then you can develop more of your content around that keyword phrase.

You'll want to create blog posts optimized for that term, use it as a hashtag on Twitter, and participate in forum chat rooms around questions and topics that use the phrase "Dog Grooming."

The knowledge you gain from a small investment in pay-per-click advertising can make all the difference. Your PPC keyword tests go a long way toward helping you plan the rest of your content marketing and may save you tens of thousands of dollars you might have spent on a campaign around "Get my dog a bath" or another term that would not have brought the kind of traffic you need.

Spy on Competitors' Ads

There's also a lot you can learn by looking at your competitors. You can research what terms your competitors are bidding on most for their PPC ads, and consider whether those keywords might benefit your own content marketing strategy. Use online tools such as these to make spying easy:

- **MixRank** (*http://www.mixrank.com*)
- **WhatRunsWhere** (*http://www.whatrunswhere.com*)
- **KeywordSpy** (*http://www.keywordspy.com*)

In addition, **Linkdex** (*http://www.linkdex.com*) can show you a map of affiliate sites that link to your competitors. Understanding what sites and types of content are being used to monetize and send traffic is a great tipoff for potential content that could be part of your next campaign.

5) Beyond the Search Engines

There are many ways to get seeds for your next content marketing campaign beyond researching on search engines. Social media, news headlines, trending topics, customer questions, your old content and even life inside your company can all be good sources of ideas as well.

Social Media

Social media sites let you keep your ear to the ground, speak out on your business topics, and interact with your target audience. As you keep tabs on what's being said about your brand and your subject matter, you'll glean lots of ideas for keywords and content.

- **Twitter:** In Twitter, searches tell you what your customers are talking about and what you might want to make content about that piggybacks on trending topics and terminology relevant to your business. Because Twitter is such a fast-moving social media tool and focuses so much on headlines and sound bites, it also gives you an ongoing crash course in the kinds of keywords your audience reacts to. So use Twitter to get an in-depth look at what people are saying around a given keyword and use that information to create content that:

  o   Solves a problem

  o   Answers a question in-depth

  o   Offers a new perspective

  o   Takes a contrary position on a prevailing view or approach that you think has a hole in it

- **Facebook:** Facebook pages are a fantastic and targeted way to understand what kind of content is resonating with your current audience and customers. If you develop a regular sharing schedule on your page of both your own and relevant content from around the web, you will notice patterns of what people comment on and share. "Likes" can be an indicator here, but the more compelling information is what people engage with through commenting and sharing. As you post content, keep track of what is being commented on and shared. Periodically review the headlines and images of your most engaging content. Any patterns you notice will be starting points for how to compose your next campaign.

- **Social Media Monitoring Tools:** Social media monitoring tools do an amazing job of tracking conversations about your company around the Internet. They can also be a powerful research tool. A tool like **Alerti** (*http://alerti.com*) can help you track your own keywords, potential keywords and the content of your competitors. From this data you will have a market-wide understanding of what content gets the most engagement and is shared the most. (See Chapter 9 for more on monitoring social media.)

Current Headlines and Trends

Sometimes you will want to tie your overall content campaign to news, upcoming events or other trending phrases that are hyper-relevant to a keyword or long-tail phrase for a short time. Looking at news blogs with large readerships is a great way to get an idea of what works. Current-news sites like the following all do a great job of publishing timely content around trends and stories as well as optimizing headlines for maximum traffic:

- **Huffington Post** (*http://www.huffingtonpost.com*)
- **The Atlantic** (*http://www.theatlantic.com*)
- **Yahoo!**'s homepage (*http://www.yahoo.com*)

Blending whatever the current headlines are focused on with your overall content marketing campaign and brand story will keep you top-of-mind and help you tap into the moment. This can make a great companion arm to the more long-term goals of your content marketing campaigns. We're not suggesting that you piggyback on a celebrity name or other topic that has nothing to do with your content. However, look for overlaps and creative tie-ins that can boost the exposure of your relevant content.

Blog Comments and Customer Service Inquiries

One of the best ways to find content ideas is to listen to actual customer requests. Pay attention to the questions that people ask your company in blog comments and customer service emails. Often these questions can lead to ideas for new content that will answer real customer needs.

What do your customers want to know more about? What is confusing to them? Is there potential for you to elaborate on a topic and turn a single page of content into a series?

Refreshing old content can be a great opportunity to get double or triple the bang for your content-creation buck.

Consider creating articles and videos based on actual questions from your target market. You could even address the person by name (for instance, "George from Pennsylvania recently asked me . . ."), or you may choose to answer the questions without identifying that the topic is derived from customer feedback. This type of customer inquiry-based content does a great job answering your buyers' questions, and also serves to get your content in front of potential customers who may have the same questions and, as a result, are able to find your brand organically through search.

Old Content Repurposed as New

The idea of taking something old and remaking it fresh works in many situations. Why not apply this "reuse, recycle" mentality to your content strategy?

Sometimes you'll be surprised to find that an article you wrote months or years ago continues to get regular traffic. Start by looking for old content that is still performing well. For example, at Bruce Clay, Inc. we recently noticed in Google Analytics reports that a 2007 blog post was still seeing a lot of search traffic. So the topic of the post is still viable and meeting a need. However, since seven years is eons in Internet time, we've slated to refresh that article and turn it into an evergreen page. (See Chapter 4 for more about creating evergreen content.)

If you can't find any good candidates of old content that's still highly trafficked, look for old content that performed well in its heyday. It may be worth creating a fresh version of the same topic that will be useful today.

> *Talking about your business can make good content if it's helpful or engaging.*

To refresh an old news article, you might only need to add an update at the top to bring the information current rather than rewrite it entirely. Or, how about doing a retrospective "look how far we've come" piece that compares where things are today to where they were then? Or it could reflect on how the news of yesteryear has informed the present.

If the content is *evergreen* (always relevant regardless of how old it is), could you use the old article as inspiration and repurpose it? Here are some ideas:

- Write a new article that approaches the topic with an alternative solution or perspective.
- Put the content into a new format, such as turning a novella-length blog post into a series of five-minute video quick tips.
- Create an infographic that illustrates the information.
- Make a white paper that expands the topic.
- Run a contest or do interviews to engage people around the topic.

Searching your archives for opportunities to refresh or repurpose old content can be a great opportunity to get double or triple the bang for your content-creation buck.

My Own Business News

Talking about yourself isn't bad when what you're talking about interests or benefits the listener. While content that's overly promotional will surely turn off a reader, talking about your business *can* make good content if it's helpful or engaging.

If you're stumped for content ideas, try turning the camera around and looking internally for inspiration. Of course, you should always verify that whatever company information you want to write about isn't confidential; to be safe, run your content ideas by your supervisor or even your legal department before making them public knowledge. But with that disclaimer aside, try looking around with fresh eyes to see what would be interesting or valuable if you were just visiting for the first time.

To prompt ideas, how about these?

- Share something that your company does internally that might teach your peers or customers something useful (to build an audience).

- Discuss your community or charitable involvement (to improve brand loyalty).

- Share a profile of one of your team leaders or a video that shows off your company culture (to boost recruitment and brand interest).

Think about what your business is doing that might be interesting to your audience. What can you write about that will help them solve a problem, learn something new or find out how to do something they don't know how to do? Topics may come from the products you create and the services you offer, but also from the way you do business, the impact you're making, or the way the industry or the future looks from your company's vantage point. When you turn those topics into content, the world may find what you have to say useful or even inspiring.

Chapter 4

Blogging: The Axis of a Content Marketing Strategy

Yes, you need a blog. In fact, it's the hub of any content marketing you hope to do. And it should be focused on furthering your business objectives.

A Brief History of Blogs

Blogging and blogs first started to spread across the Internet in the late 1990s. At that point people were still thinking of them by their original name, "web-log," and you could count the number of companies writing blog posts on one hand. It wasn't until 1998–99, when LiveJournal, TypePad and Blogger were all created, that everyone had access to this amazing outlet. Then in 2003, WordPress came along and changed the game for all of us.

Over the last 15 years, we've gone from no business having a blog to seemingly every business having a blog—sometimes more than one. Experts have been debating for years questions like: *Does my business need a blog? What should a business blog be about? What belongs on a business blog? How can my business get better at blogging?*

It used to be enough to start a blog and try things out — it meant you were ahead of the curve. But today the facts are in, and blogs are proven business assets. According to a 2013 report on the state of inbound marketing, having a successful blog is a key indicator that a company has effective inbound marketing:

> **" *79% of companies who have a blog reported a positive ROI for inbound marketing this year, compared with just 20% of those companies who did not have a blog.*"**

– HubSpot, "2013 State of Inbound Marketing Report"[1]

What we are seeing now with blogs is the further convergence of substance and style. In the past, businesses could get by with something that was good in one area but not as good in another. Some businesses created beautiful blogs that fell short on copy. Others had great writing but couldn't figure out how to add quality design. Both writing and design are important for a content marketing campaign, and it takes both to have a successful blog.

The blog you create becomes a critical axis for your content marketing, and it must support your brand. That means it needs to be both good-looking and full of high quality content. Your blog is the single most important hub of activity for your web presence.

And at the same time, don't limit your blogging to just your home turf. It's equally important to speak to your target audience on other blogs that they read. Guest posting and having your face, name, brand and content appear on neutral publications legitimizes you. It tells customers that other people recognize you as an authority figure or thought leader in your industry. It builds trust, reinforces relationships and evangelizes your brand to new audience members. With so many blogs out there and blogging such a powerful media force, you have a lot of opportunities to make your brand's voice heard.

We've established that *whether* you need a blog is no longer the right question. Let's move on to the right question: *How can you use blogs to meet your business objectives?*

Making a Company Blog Pay for Itself

The blog on your company website acts as the hub for any content marketing campaign. Your blog enables you to consistently give something to your customers and the community. It builds trust and familiarity with your brand. And it functions as part of your sales funnel anytime a prospect visits your website looking for more.

A blog is an investment. It takes commitment to produce quality content regularly and manage an active blog. But consider the upside: you have total control over what content gets published on your blog. This is where your voice will be strongest, because it is your home turf. When you invest in your blog, you are building your foundation.

How can you make that investment pay off? Here we'll cover marketing and search engine optimization best practices you can apply to create a successful company blog.

Titles: The All-Important Crown for My Content

In content marketing, titles are king-makers.

Titles catch a reader's eye, drive traffic, and are sometimes the only thing people read closely in your article!

As with all content you create, communicating clearly should be the first priority when crafting article titles. Of course you want your title to stand out from the crowd, but first and foremost titles need to effectively convey subject matter to human readers and search engine spiders.

How to Write a Great Title

Article titles carry a lot of weight with users and search engine spiders. This critical marketing element can influence a search engine to move your article up or down the ranks, and a searcher to either read your article or skip it.

In SEO land, the word *title* primarily refers to the `<title>` tag located in the HTML code of a page (see Figure 4.1). Most people, however, say "title" to refer to the large headline above an article (which technically is the *heading*). And now that content moves so fluidly from platform to platform, one could argue that the title is not just the original tag or heading but also its morphed versions as it travels around the web — a condensed phrase for Twitter, an intriguing comment on Reddit, a personalized headline on Facebook, and so forth.

In a minute we'll talk about title techniques that can help blog content go viral. But to start, let's cover best practices for writing *any* title effectively.

1) **Make your title concise, specific and benefit-driven.** Modern Internet users want everything immediately; they will likely go elsewhere if you make them work too hard. Blog readers don't have time to unpack your pun or figure out what you're trying to imply. They want to know what an article offers and whether it's what they need, right away. So craft article titles that are to-the-point and easily understood. Here are some tips:

   o **Length:** Keep your title around 8 words or less.

   o **Numbers:** Starting with a number tends to attract interest and communicate how comprehensive the article will be, such as *"100 SEO Tips for Beginners."* As a bonus, numbers get sorted before letters when alphabetized, so this can be an easy way to rise to the top of a list.

   o **Benefits:** User-benefit wording like *"How to"* or *"What to Avoid"* quickly gives your reader a clear idea of what the article will cover and the approach you'll take.

2) **Optimize your title for search.** Search engines look at an article's title to determine how relevant it is to specific search queries and subjects. Accordingly, writing your title clearly, concisely and with a keyword can boost your article's SERP rank. Search engine spiders do not have time or technical ability to figure out what your witty, unclear blog title is trying to convey.

   o **Use keywords people search for:** Google pays special attention to your article title to figure out what your content is about, so be strategic about the words. Always perform keyword research to understand how your target market searches for content, then incorporate phrases that ideally have high search volume but low competition.

     For instance, you may find that "video SEO" has significantly more monthly searches than "video optimization." In this case, since both phrases convey your subject matter equally well, you would want to use the language that your target market most commonly uses and title your article *"10 Video SEO Tips,"* rather than *"10 Video Optimization Tips."*

     Using the **Google Keyword Planner** and other popular tools (see Chapter 3 for more on keyword research tools), you can find great ideas for blog post titles that people are searching for. Spending some time reading the blogs your competitors write, researching trending topics, and looking at your own blog analytics will also give you great titles and keywords for your content.

   o **Go for clarity:** Don't shoot yourself in the foot trying to be overly clever. Be clear instead, both for the spider's and the user's benefit. For example, scrap *"Why You CAN Judge a Blog Post by Its Cover"* for the more straightforward *"5 Tips to Create Better Blog Post Titles."*

3) **Write to inspire action.** The action you're after may be a click-through, a social media share or even just the act of reading to the next paragraph. But since an article's Title tag almost always shows up as the big blue link in search results, writing it deserves your attention and marketer's skill (see Figure 4-1).

Focusing on clarity doesn't mean you stop trying to write titles that are engaging and energized. There might be a dozen other articles on the exact same topic; if yours makes it to page one, what will make a searcher click your post rather than the others? What words will entice someone to choose your article from the dozens streaming through their Twitter feed, email bin, Facebook wall and so on?

Take time to really consider how to get that perfect balance of clarity, optimization and individuality. And don't be afraid to show your brand personality when appropriate.

For example, a title like "*5 Guest Blogging Tips*" is a great straightforward option, but you may also consider the benefit-driven but slightly more enticing "*How Guest Blogging Helped Get Me 8 Million Visitors.*"

Figure 4-1: The Title tag in your blog post's HTML code usually becomes the big blue link in search results.

How to Make Titles Go Viral

Murray has a friend from his home town of Cambridge named Sue Keogh (*http://sookio.com*). A former editor on the homepage teams for Yahoo! and AOL, she worked specifically on content for the "Featured" box on the homepage, which is a key driver of traffic around each of those portals. Besides writing body text and picking attention-grabbing pictures, her job was to optimize the words in the headlines. The simple fact that they had teams working round the clock on this speaks volumes about the importance of titles and the effect they can have on traffic and the bottom line.

Keogh says they could see millions more clicks and shares on titles that were properly optimized.

She's the one who first suggested that you might call a blog post one thing on your blog but then share it with a different title or indexing text in other social media. So we asked her to share some of what she thinks about titles and how to harness their power.

Here are some of her **key tips on writing titles that help make your content go viral.**

What is the Purpose of a Title?

Titles have a big job to do. The title's main purposes are to:

- Make your content stand out
- Attract your target audience
- Make your content more likely to be shared

A good title can be very persuasive. It can get people to read your content or click your link. Sometimes people will retweet a link on the strength of the title alone without even reading the article.

What If I Don't Have a Good Title?

If your title is weak, people won't be curious enough to read or share the content. And all your hard work creating the content will be wasted.

Since most people read *only* the headline, you have to make it good. So avoid abstract titles and tell the reader exactly what the post is about. Otherwise they're not going to open, read or share.

Title Formulas that Work

When creating your blog post titles, why not borrow formulas that have proven track records? Here are a few you can try.

- **Teaser text:** A technique that continues to make curious Yahoo! readers click on an endless stream of featured homepage images is teasing the content. Write a short title that hints at what makes the article helpful, interesting, controversial or funny. Just don't give the game away! Keogh also states an important caution for would-be teasers:

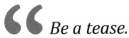 *Be a tease.*
   But don't promise what you can't deliver."

   – Sue Keogh[2]

- **Question words:** Using "W" words like *who, what, when, where* and *why* help signpost content. For example, a title like *"Things Apple Didn't Talk About at WWDC"* would be improved if rewritten like this: *"What Apple Didn't Announce at WWDC and Why."*

- **Number+:** Smashing Magazine came up with a simple formula for writing titles that you can see commonly used on sites like Buzzfeed, which deliver a continual stream of highly share-worthy content. Here's the formula:

   Number + adjective + item + sticky message

   Applying that formula to a blog post, you could get *"83 Beautiful WordPress Themes You (Probably) Haven't Seen."*

Evergreen Content: Making Long-lived Posts

As mentioned in Chapter 3, *evergreen content* is content that will always be relevant to your readers.

Creating evergreen content as part of your ongoing content marketing is a great opportunity to take a deep dive into your business objectives. When you think about writing evergreen blog posts for content marketing, think about the key, timeless topics that your customers will always be interested in.

For example, if you have a dog grooming company, a blog post titled *"12 Simple Dog Grooming Secrets That Will Save You Time"* would make good evergreen content. It's a timeless topic that will always be relevant to one of your main target markets, people who are interested in dog grooming.

Tips for Creating Evergreen Content

- **Choose timeless topics:** Write timeless blog posts based on topics that will build trust with your readers and, accordingly, bring them closer to spending money with your business. For instance, our evergreen dog grooming article could be a great way to draw in leads. People who are interested in saving time when they groom their dog may also be interested in hiring a professional groomer at some point. Because your article helped them, they may develop a trust in your brand which will make them more likely to turn to you when they are ready to pay for professional help.

- **Build on your popular posts:** Look at your blog posts that are performing well to see if there are any opportunities for you to create related evergreen content and link from your established post to these new posts. This can be a good way for you to target and nurture a new content cluster, strategically transfer PageRank from your authoritative web page to fresh pages, develop your on-page optimization and improve your SERP rank.

For example, if you have an evergreen blog article titled *"How to Start a Blog"* that has developed authority and SERP rank over the years, you might find it beneficial to create and link to three additional evergreen content pages that explain how to optimize a blog, how to write for a blog and how to use WordPress. From those three new pages you can also link back to the original *"How to Start a Blog"* article, and each blog post can link to one another, further emphasizing the connectedness and relevance of the pages.

Including links to related content within posts is also a great way to give your visitor's more content that is likely to help them, which is great for user experience and an excellent way to keep visitors on your website longer.

TIPS: *For a refresher on content clusters and how to create them, see Chapter 2. For an explanation of PageRank transfer, see* http://www.bruceclay.com/blog/2013/09/what-is-pagerank.

- **Update old posts:** Use analytics reports to identify older posts that are performing well months or even years after their publish date. If appropriate, consider updating these posts to make them more relevant to a current audience.

As long as you don't change the topic and simply *update* the post rather than *rewrite* the article entirely, updating your older content will keep your authority and SERP rank intact while improving user experience. Rewriting could potentially change your SERP ranking by changing how relevant search engines find the page's new content.

For instance, say you are a paint distributor and you have a blog post titled *"The Best Paint Brand for You"* that has been performing well for years. Unfortunately, the paint brand you mention in your post (which, let's assume, was written four years ago) has recently been discontinued. Since the page has been around for so long, it has authority and SERP rank for a query people search for often. This means your outdated content is being seen by thousands of people, and what should be thousands of leads has turned into thousands of unsatisfied bounces. One way to solve this problem would be to update the post so that the focus is on a "best paint brand" that is currently available for purchase.

Evergreen Content Keeps on Giving

Evergreen content is like a workhorse that never quits. These enduring blog posts help you build content clusters, improve SERP rank and bring you traffic day in and day out through organic search, links from other blogs and websites, and referrals. Plus, watching your evergreen content to discover which types get the most traffic can offer you great insight into what your target audience responds to.

Since evergreen topics are timeless, creating a bank of evergreen content ideas can also be a great solution to writer's block. On a rainy day when you're low on new releases or news, you'll have a good resource to pull ideas from.

Trending Topics: Riding the Popularity Wave

By nature, blogs work beautifully with short-term, newsy, intriguing content. Topics popular in the moment can be quickly covered and easily published within a blog format. As a wave of public interest swells about a celebrity, event or other topic, there's room for marketers to talk about the trending topic and ride the wave for a short time.

Some trending topics seem spontaneous, like someone jumping up on a table at a party and singing an unexpected song. Others you can see coming because they are based on a popular upcoming event. Either way, these topics have their moment in the sun and then drift into relative obscurity. Any content marketing campaign can expand its reach by creating timely content or even a separate campaign around these trending topics.

How to Create Content on a Trending Topic

Content focused on a trending topic will often reach a big audience quickly and bring you a spike in traffic. And the trending news need not be yours. Like a surfer catching a wave, your content can be picked up and carried on the wave of a bigger topic.

This works because you are tapping into an audience for a particular topic and entering their conversation in a timely manner with just the right content. The key is to do it in a way that brings people in because of the trending topic, but hooks them with a reason to stick with you, thus moving them down your content marketing funnel.

Where to Find Trending Topics

Current events are a great source of trending topics, especially if those events have some obvious tie-in to the mission of your company. If you are going to work with trending topics, you must be very agile in what you are doing and the types of content you can create. For that reason, this tactic works better in small and medium-sized businesses than it does in larger corporations, where many layers of required approvals can slow down the content-creation process.

In addition to news sources, another great source for trending-topic ideas is **Google Trends** (*http://www.google.com/trends*). This free tool lets you see top-searched topics and even enter your own terms to see how they are trending over time (see Figure 4-2).

Even some of the more popular content portals such as **Yahoo!** (*http://www.yahoo.com*), **AOL** (*http://www.aol.com*) and others make good sources. You will see how they always hit their content stories to catch trending topics.

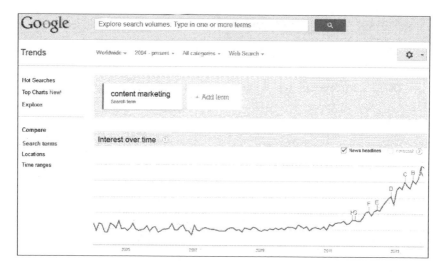

Figure 4-2: Google Trends shows search volume over time. This graph shows the recent rise in popularity of "content marketing."

Example of Trending Topics in Action

A dedicated microsite was set up in 2011 to monitor the social media buzz circulating around the 2012 U.S. presidential election. Creators were the Meltwater Group and the public relations giant Edelman. In their research they had found a correlation between people who liked political analysis and people who bought social media monitoring software, so they designed a site to attract them.

In a news release announcing the site, Meltwater's marketing and communications director said, "Meltwater Election Buzz will provide a one-of-a-kind resource for press, bloggers, political analysts and everyday voters to glean key insights into news and social media trends around the 2012 election."[3] The site enabled Meltwater to produce content, including blog posts, to ride every wave of the presidential campaign for 12 months.

Content Marketing: Repurposing Content & Collective Social Wisdom

By Lee Odden

One of the great talents of an effective content marketer is the ability to re-create, or as my pal Ann Handley says, "reimagine," content.

Many companies don't have the resources to create anything new. Yet many companies are sitting on all types of content and digital assets that could repackaged, re-purposed or curated into usefulness as a marketing asset. We recently worked with a Fortune 100 company to bring over 140 videos online using topical themes according to specific vertical markets and of course, keywords for optimization. Images, text, audio and video are all potential candidates for offline to online repurposing.

There are any number of practical reasons to reuse content including:

Efficiency — With a hub and spoke model for publishing optimized, social content there exists a number of repurposing opportunities. There's an efficiency to that publishing model because you're planning in advance to repurpose content in different formats for different channels.

A classic example is to announce a product. The core content of the announcement is the hub (company website or blog) and surrounding it are social spokes and other channels for promotion which might include a press release version of the blog post, a video of a product manager explaining the product or interviewing a client beta tester, images of the product itself and the product being used, tweets, updates, presentations, specification documents, promotional documents and media, and so on.

Short Attention Span — Social content consumers not only get distracted easily but have short attention spans. Posting a tweet with a link to the content you're promoting could be scheduled to repost 2–3 more times in a 24-hour period, with each tweet taking a slightly different angle on the story. Not only can additional variations inspire interest but also RT's and shares.

Building SEO Relevancy — We target about 20 core keyword phrases with this blog, yet over 20,000 unique keyword phrases are used to drive visitors here every month. When SEO and content marketing strategies work together, repurposing content means additional SEO assets to attract search traffic on many different variations of a theme.

Google reports that 16 percent of the queries it sees every day have never been seen before. That means building out a content footprint that represents a diversity of keywords on a theme will help a company attract an audience that is actively looking beyond the broad (and more competitive) phrases that everyone else is optimizing for.

Content Marketing: Repurposing Content & Collective Social Wisdom
(continued)

Personalize for Verticals or Customer Segments — If your product/service targets different vertical markets, there's no reason not to craft a core message that's then customized for each industry and audience segment so you can pitch as a byline article or guest blog post.

Using a template, you might have customizable expressions or paragraphs according to specific verticals or customer segments that accentuate unique benefits, data and customer goals. Then a skilled copywriter would review and make final adjustments versus writing from scratch about something that is essentially the same but meant for a slightly different market.

The cost and difficulty of scaling content creation has boosted the desire to find something that taps into the stores of existing content and digital assets. Creative content repurposing is an effective way to do that.

Lee Odden is the author of *Optimize* and CEO of @TopRank Online Marketing, focused on search, social media, PR and content marketing. A version of this article was originally published at *http://www.toprankblog.com/2012/07/content-marketing-collective-wisdom*.

Guest Blogging: A Way to Reach New Audiences

Guest blogging allows you to feature other writers' original content on your blog, and vice versa. Once your blog has an audience, others will be willing to write for it. This source of content benefits you because a guest post:

- Demands less of your time and resources, since you don't have to do the writing

- Grows your readership and introduces your brand to a new audience

- Integrates your blog into a new network of sharing and visibility, especially if the guest author proceeds to share the post socially

- Adds credibility to your blog, since an expert guest is willing to be associated with it.

Inviting someone to write for your blog is also a powerful way to leverage existing relationships and expand your reach to audiences elsewhere on the Internet. You always need to be building new relationships online. Look for people whose articles are capturing the audience you want to reach. Your job is to reach out to those bloggers and build a relationship. A great ways to do that is to offer them what bloggers always need — content. Suggest a cooperative agreement in which you write a post for their blog and they write one for yours. If you are a good writer, you may be able to reach audiences many times the size or your own blog's, even reaching millions of people.

In addition, look for opportunities to write guest posts for high-value, relevant blogs. If a friend recommends a product to you, it's statistically proven that you will value that recommendation more highly than an advertisement you happen to see. This is because we naturally put more faith in the recommendations of people we respect than in what people (or companies) say about themselves.

> *The main reason you should guest blog is to reach a new audience, not improve your search engine ranking.*

It works the same way in blogging. If a company or blogger publishes your content on their blog, it's a vote of confidence in you and what you have to say. This can work powerfully to expand your readership, get your content in front of more people, drive traffic back to your own site or wherever else you want traffic, forward your business objectives, and build relationships in the process.

Guest Blogging and SEO

The main reason you should guest blog is to reach a new audience, not to improve your search engine ranking.

In the past, guest blogging for someone else's blog was seen as a good SEO technique for creating backlinks to your website that would build your PageRank. Not so anymore. In fact, *search engines may actually penalize your site* if they suspect that you paid for those links. For this reason, Google recently advised bloggers to be careful when guest blogging.

How to Safely Guest Post on Someone Else's Blog

Here are a few guidelines to keep you safe when guest blogging, based on a recent video by Matt Cutts, head of Google's search quality team.[4]

- **Write on a relevant subject:** Guest posts look suspicious to search engines when they don't match the subject of the blog itself. If you're posting on a plumber's blog, your content should be about plumbing, not payday loans.

- **Links should NOT be keyword-stuffed:** Contrary to SEO advice of the past, you don't want to use keywords in the *anchor text* (i.e., words that can be clicked) of links pointing back to your website. To be safe, include only one link back to your site, perhaps in the short author's bio, and use your name, your brand or your website URL as anchor text. Stuffing links with keywords (e.g., "no-fee guaranteed payday loans") can look like spam.

- **Make unique content:** Be careful not to spin the same content across many websites. When you offer to write for someone else, give them original, quality content they can put up with confidence. The search engines filter out duplicated content.

- **Guest blog in moderation:** Don't make guest posting your full-time job, as a flood of guest posts looks like spam. An occasional guest appearance, however, looks natural and boosts your credibility as an authority.

Creating Guest Blogging Partnerships

Just as it is valuable to guest post on someone else's blog, it can also be valuable to host guest bloggers. As you blog for others and others begin to blog for you, blogging partnerships can naturally form. If you maintain those partnerships, you can create many ongoing opportunities to help each other with your respective content marketing campaigns.

One thing many people don't realize when pitching a guest blog post is that those sites want content that electrifies their audience.

Five Tips for Establishing Blogging Partnerships that Work

1) **Plan new topics:** When you begin a blogging partnership, discuss with your partner what he or she plans on covering. You'll want to make sure your partner is blogging about topics that you haven't already covered in the blog yourself. If they have a fresh perspective on a previously covered topic, consider giving the go-ahead for a blog post that approaches the subject from a new angle.

2) **Give guidelines:** Ideally, provide your partner with editorial or style guidelines. If you don't have any, take the time to create some so that all of your blog contributors are on the same page when it comes to style, tone and intention.

3) **Set length:** Provide your partner with a desired word-count range up front. There is no way for him to know you are expecting 500 words and not 2,000 unless you tell him. The key here is to be as clear as possible from the very beginning. The more communication, the better — that way there are no unpleasant surprises for you, your partner or your editorial team.

4) **Communicate as needed:** If you find yourself needing to make major editorial changes, don't be afraid to offer constructive criticism at the beginning of your relationship so that the two of you can get the intended tone and direction down earlier rather than later.

5) **Thank them:** Remember to be supportive of your partners throughout the editorial process and make sure to let them know you are grateful for their work. This may seem trite, but remember that relationship building is an essential piece of this partnership. You need your partners to enjoy working with you; sometimes simply letting someone know you appreciate the work they are doing goes a long way.

Pitching a Guest Blog Partnership

Building new blogging partnerships and getting your content onto new blogs can be challenging. It's the online equivalent of in-person networking meetings. As such, it helps to have a friend or fellow blogger you already have a relationship with to introduce you to a new blogger. That's the foundation of the social web — people introducing web-savvy people to other web-savvy people.

One of the things that many people do not realize when pitching to publications is that those sites want content that electrifies their audience. The trick is to blend what energizes your own target audience with what is valuable to theirs.

If you want XYZ publication to carry your content, then you need to think from XYZ's perspective. Ask yourself, what will excite XYZ's readers and get them to engage with the content? The publication will, in one way or another, generate income if readers experience that personal connection with the content. The more popular the content, the more it will be shared and liked, the more traffic the publication will have, and the more advertising page views they will get. You need to figure out how your story can best engage their audience and get shared.

You're creating content at the convergence of what you want to talk about and what will excite the audience where you are guest posting.

One way to pique a publication's interest is to have a timely story on a trending topic with a great headline. If you are able to supply publications with great content that gets lots of social shares and readers, then you will get the opportunity to work with them to produce lots of content and reach a bigger and bigger audience. There is also the opportunity to show this content to other publishing sites and climb up the tree of publications.

Large publications want writers who know how to create good content and can bring an audience. They also want someone who is an expert to be the expert for them. A good way to start guest posting is to write for some medium-sized sites in your subject area. Especially when your posts generate a lot of social shares and comments, you'll be able to work your way up to larger publications with a larger audience and readership.

When you get a piece in a great publication, do all you can to promote it like crazy and demonstrate that you have a strong following. There is nothing worse for a publication than to go to the trouble of publishing a guest post and then have the author of the piece not even bother to promote it. In essence, if you do it well the first time, they'll want you to come back and post again.

Guest posts lay the foundation for an ongoing blogging partnership. You'll also expand your potential audience for future content marketing.

If you can deliver quality content through guest posts, you'll lay the foundation for an ongoing blogging partnership. You'll also expand your potential audience for future content marketing.

Getting the Press and Blogs to Write about Me

Getting other people to write about you fuels any content marketing campaign. You might get classic press, with people covering your campaign because it makes a compelling story. Or you can integrate your content with what the readers of another blog are interested in, similar to the approach we recommended with guest blogging.

How to Get Noticed

Making an offer: There are ways to make it easier and more attractive for other bloggers to write about you as part of your content marketing campaign. People respond better when you offer them something, rather than just asking for something or immediately going for the sale. Reach out with an offer to write a guest post, or invite them to guest post or contribute a quote for a post you are writing. This gets them engaging with your content and your blog, which will make them more familiar with you and how you operate.

Connecting in person: The absolute best way to get people to write about you is to meet them in person.

- The website **MeetUp** (*http://www.meetup.com*) can help you find local media or blogging events.

- Conferences and live events about your topic let you make great connections in person.

- There may also be a social scene connected with your industry where you can meet reporters and bloggers. This can be tricky, as you'll need to be sensitive to the fact that they may consider themselves off duty and might not want your pitch.

Social media outreach: If you cannot meet reporters and bloggers in real life, try to connect with them through social media. The incredible opportunity here is that on social media, there are no assistants in the way — most people use Twitter, LinkedIn and other networks as themselves. This means you have a chance to make direct contact. Be personable, but don't stalk them! To make a good first impression, share and comment on some of their content, and try to engage around something they're interested in.

Paid content: You can pay to publish a content series on a website or sponsor some content. As long as the hosting site discloses it is sponsored content and any links back to your site are *nofollowed* (i.e., not meant to pass authority or PageRank), then there will be no conflict with it. Not just small sites, but even large sites like Mashable, have run sponsored content before. Murray in particular has worked with publications to create sponsored content series with great effect for clients.

Commenting: Commenting can be an incredibly effective way of reaching your audience. Press coverage is a challenge to get no matter who you are. But there is a good chance that the publications you wish would write about you are frequently carrying content similar to yours. Why not let yourself be known in the comments?

Kym McNicholas, executive producer of PandoDaily and a reporter at Forbes, recently said that making great comments on a relevant article can put your name in front of the people who are reading that article, which is your target audience.

In a similar way, when a publication writes about your area of expertise or about one of your competitors, they may not want to cover the same topic again very soon. Adding value to an existing article through a comment is a great way to put your name in the mind of the reader, who is already reading about a company or subject in your field. Do not bash the competition or try and sell what you do too hard; just make a great comment and be part of that content.

Following: Finally, following your competitors and topics throughout the media channels gives you an idea of who has written about your subject recently. One convenient way to monitor news across the web is to set up **Google Alerts**

(*http://www.google.com/alerts*), which will email you updates of all the latest news for any topics you specify. Once you have good media sites and blogs on your radar, monitor what they post in your subject area. Blogs that haven't covered your topic in a while may be more interested in writing about you.

Chapter Notes

[1] HubSpot, "2013 State of Inbound Marketing Annual Report," page 85. <http://offers.hubspot.com/2013-state-of-inbound-marketing>

[2] Sue Keogh, "Tweets that Travel: Seven tips for viral writing." <http://www.slideshare.net/sookio/tweets-the-travel-how-to-write-viral-copy>

[3] Kimling Lam, "Photo Release – Meltwater Launches 2012 Presidential Election Social Buzz Monitoring Website." 7 November 2011. <http://globenewswire.com/news-release/2011/11/07/460742/237350/en/Photo-Release-Meltwater-Launches-2012-Presidential-Election-Social-Buzz-Monitoring-Website.html>

[4] Matt Cutts, "How can I guest blog without it appearing as if I paid for links?" Video from GoogleWebmasterHelp. 16 October 2013. <http://www.youtube.com/watch?v=OGieiNe6RL4>

Chapter 5

Curation: I Don't Have to Be the Expert to Be the Go-To

What Is Content Curation?

Content curation is the process of finding, organizing, contextualizing and sharing relevant, quality content with the right audience. In the context of content marketing, it's also about curating and sharing content that will advance your business objectives, whether that means becoming a thought-leader, generating leads or expanding your online network.

The beauty of curation is that you don't have to be an expert to become a go-to source. You can be a critical part of the conversation about a topic or a niche in your field without the pressure of creating expert content. If you are good at finding and sharing relevant content that furthers your business goals, that can be just as valuable as creating it from scratch.

With so much content being created and shared every day, content creation is fast becoming a tremendous way to generate traffic and show that you understand what truly great content looks like.

Why Curate Content?

Why would any business spend time curating content instead of focusing that time on creating original content? It's a fair question. The answers vary depending on what kind of content marketing campaign you are engaged in, but there are many reasons.

1) Build Relationships with Fans and Media Partners

Any content marketing campaign will involve building and reinforcing relationships with people who are active online. Curating content that those people create is a fantastic way to build the foundation or reinforce those important relationships.

With fans or customers, curating content helps establish a more personal relationship across a gap between brand and customer that is still typically a wide one. This kind of act still makes a huge impact for the person whose content ends up on a business's web presence.

With the press and blogging partners, when you choose to curate content they created you enhance the relationship you already have, especially if it is outside of a current contract. Often the people whose work you curate will notice that you've shared their content, which can make them notice your website, blog, and so forth. Then — if they like what they see — they may include your original content in future curated pieces that they put together.

There's a right way and a wrong way to curate other people's content. Search engine guidelines and even ethics come into play.

Think of this exchange not so much as a "you scratch my back, I'll scratch yours" arrangement where friends link arbitrarily to friends. Instead, consider it a "you have what I need, and I have what you need" exchange that benefits all parties involved, including both websites' target markets.

When done with finesse, this inbound-linking chain reaction can significantly increase your relevance to target keyword phrases, inspire improved SERP rankings and boost traffic numbers.

2) Establish My Company as a Thought Leader

If you want to be known as a thought leader in your niche, the currency you need to trade in is information. You will be known for what you talk about.

We all experience this in our day-to-day lives. If you want a new book, you know which friend to go to for a book recommendation. That friend didn't write those books, but because the friend constantly talks about books, you consider him or her an expert in that field. When you need a new book, what that friend recommends carries weight.

Keep in mind how your curation selections reflect on you or your brand, and you'll avoid having to backpedal or remove feet from mouths.

You want to be the one people turn to when they are looking for a recommendation, a project or reliable information. As a curator, you can save your audience a lot of time and effort by sorting out the best sources of information, and adding a comment or insight that will be seen as connected to the great content you are sharing.

A great example of this is O'Reilly Media (*http://www.oreilly.com*), an organization that curates content through both its online blog and hosted conferences (see example in Figure 5-1).

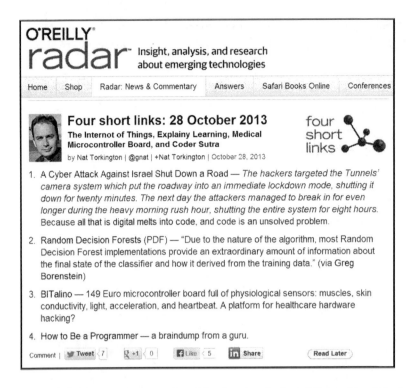

Figure 5-1: This post does curation right: four hand-selected links with original commentary that adds value.

3) Become a Destination

If one of your content marketing goals is to bring more traffic to your website, curating quality content can go a long way toward achieving it. Being a destination for a certain kind of content, as HubSpot (*http://www.hubspot.com*) is for inbound marketing, will raise your standing in your field. When you hand-pick content from around the web and then add value by curating it with your own comments, that can have SEO benefits that lead to more traffic from organic search, as well.

People at all levels of a company read blogs and use social media, so being a destination where people go to find the newest information is a powerful role. Not only does it bring you web traffic, but also it has ripple benefits throughout your interactions with anyone in the field. Your name will carry more weight, and people will want to be included in the content you are curating.

Curating Content, the Right Way

Curated content will hold up those you want to highlight and bring in those you want to influence. For these reasons, it needs to be highly targeted content. While it can be tempting to use curating content as a chance to spotlight your friends, more is at stake.

There's also a right way and a wrong way to curate other people's content. Search engine guidelines and even ethics come into play. From an SEO perspective, you need to know what *not* to do as well as how to curate content that will benefit your audience and your business.

Curating to a Blog

Your own blog is the ideal place to bring together the best of what you find across the Internet, in terms of getting the most traffic value for your effort. The key is to curate in a targeted way that supports your business objectives. Keep your curated blog content focused, rather than simply bringing together a lot of content that relates to the same general topic.

For example, finding and sharing articles about "marketing" or "sales" would be too broad. Narrow your field of content to curate. It will not only make your work easier to manage, but also allow your expertise to be that much more laser-focused.

> *Curation is ... strategically identifying resources ... and then digging around for or soliciting the content you need to tell your story.*

Curating content from within a narrow niche lets people and search engines easily grasp what you're an expert about. If you curate content as part of a thought leadership objective in a general field such as "marketing," for instance, people and search engines will pass over your site among the crowd. However, if you curate from a more specific niche like "affiliate marketing," people will have a better idea of what to expect from you. If you narrow it even further to "sports merchandise affiliate marketing" or even "basketball merchandise affiliate marketing," you will have less competition in your niche and a much better chance of becoming a go-to source (see Figure 5-2).

Figure 5-2: Targeting a narrower topic gives you a better chance to be the expert.

Potential customers or clients are more likely to be impressed with your knowledge and approach if you focus on one specific area, as well. Based on what they've seen already, they may ask if you do work in other areas. This scenario is far more likely than having prospective customers see your general knowledge and then take the time to dig down into which specific specialties you are truly an expert in.

At the heart of it, curation is all about selecting a topic your audience will find valuable, strategically identifying resources that can help you deliver that content, and then digging around for or soliciting the content you need to tell your story. To help you strategize, we've laid out some blog curation approaches to consider.

Five Ways to Curate Content for a Blog

1) **Create collections of articles to teach or illustrate points:** Create blog posts that list some of the best content out there for a specific context. For example, creating a post called the *"10 Best Examples of XYZ in 2013"* can be a great way to close out the year. This kind of roundup post allows

you to highlight the posts you have seen that do a great job with a specific topic you also cover.

Another angle you could take would be to make word count the defining curation factor, condensing and summarizing content into bite-size reads. For example, "*Quick Read: 6 Must-Read Articles on XYZ in 100 Words or Less.*"

2) **Leverage conference and event attendance:** Many industries are fast-paced with year-round conferences and expos. Use this industry-wide interest to curate lists of conference opportunities that will help people in specific niche industries. For example, you could write a post that pulls together the "*Top 5 Conferences for Windows App Developers*" or "*10 Essential Copywriting Conferences.*"

    Also take advantage of the abundance of conferences by creating or curating live conference coverage. This is especially possible in the marketing industry, where the front seats at keynotes and sessions are often filled with livebloggers, fingers flying over their keyboards, reporting the speaker's words in almost real time. If you don't have the resources to liveblog an event yourself, stay connected and curate liveblogs and other conference coverage to make a blog post like "*PubCon 2013: Liveblog Roundup*" or "*SMX Advanced 2013 Recap: 32 Takeaways.*"[1]

3) **Curate user-generated content and have your readers write content for you:** Do you have an active blog or social media community? Are your community members asking great questions? And better yet, are they also answering those questions? Use the words that come straight from the proverbial horse's mouth and curate a post that brings together some great questions and the answers the community has provided. An example title might be: "*You Said It: 5 Great Affiliate Marketing Questions Answered.*" Remember when we said that curation builds relationships with the people whose content you curate? Highlighting

user-generated content is a great opportunity to give pats on the back and really build relationships with the people who sometimes matter the most — your social community of regular patrons and brand loyalists.

Another way to leverage user-generated content is to decide on a topic that would be of interest to you and your audience — either something in the news or a cornerstone of your business — and ask your community what they think about it. You can ask for 140 characters on Twitter, or you can have people submit paragraphs in the comments section of your blog. Using this technique you'll need some time to let the responses trickle in and then put them together, but the beauty of it is that you can be working on other things while the content is more or less writing itself.

4) **Use curation to give an unbiased 360-degree perspective:** Are there any hot topics in your field that merit analysis from multiple angles? How about curating multiple opinions on a situation or issue in one post? Using collections of other people's articles to tell a story showcases their many different perspectives. Use curation to give your reader both (or all) sides of the story in a one-stop-shop format.

5) **Don't automate your curated blog posts:** This caution comes specifically from Google, with SEO in mind.2 Some websites try to take the easy route and automate curation. Using RSS feeds or other technology, they automatically find web sources that mention a particular word or phrase, then spit out a list of links, snippets or even whole content duplications as their own work. This "content," which may or may not relate to the site, lacks any commentary or added value. That is not content curation. Auto-generating links or duplicating content will not win you readers and could earn you search engine penalties. Take the time to hand-pick relevant content and add value to it through your original comments or analysis.

Curating to Social Media Channels

Sharing consistently good content on social media can be both challenging and time-consuming. That said, the great thing about social media networks is that they are inherently conversational, and as such, perfect for sharing — or "curating" — news, tips, images and other interesting content you find. Think of it as two friends talking, and one of them says, "I read a great article today. You gotta check it out."

People have said for years that you should think of the content you push out on social media channels as cocktail party conversation, and this analogy is still true to this day. No one wants to hang out with that guy who only talks about himself all the time, and no one wants to engage with a social media channel that is posting content that looks like a one-man, self-promotion feed.

Curating content is a subtle art, and when done right, it can actually give your followers a better sense of your brand personality, your interests, your endorsements, and how active you are in your niche community. In other words, it's a clever way — when done right! — *to talk about yourself without actually talking about yourself.*

Four Tips for Successful Social Media Content Curation

There's a lot of content in the world, which means content curators are faced with quite a decision to make when choosing what content to curate. Here are four tips to help you get the most out of your social media content curation.

1) **To thine own self be true — know your voice and personality:** Think through how the content you put into the world represents you and your brand personality. If you have more than one person posting on behalf of your brand, it is critical to establish a brand style guide that outlines the appropriate voice, style and personality. As mentioned, the content you curate represents you. It represents your thoughts and affinities, and curating content is often viewed as an endorsement of ideas or

opinions. Make sure everyone is on the same page regarding how to handle topics your brand has no opinion on (such as politics, religion or industry drama). Keep in mind how your curation selections reflect on you or your brand, and you'll avoid having to backpedal or remove feet from mouths.

2) **Know your audience:** As with any content creation, it's critical to know your audience when you are curating content. You want your curated content to pique their interest and make your followers relate to you and feel like they're learning more about you. Ideally, this interaction isn't contrived, and the common interests you share with your followers will generate actual relationships.

   Use your demographics data to understand what your target audience prefers (knowing that this will vary somewhat by social media platform). Keep in mind:

   - What they like
   - What they need to know
   - Their sense of humor
   - Their word-count preferences
   - Pop culture references they will get
   - Topics to avoid (sensitive subjects)
   - What they have already heard about way too much
   - How much context they need

3) **Know your networks:** It is extremely critical to understand that all social networks are not created equal, and that each of your networks will have unique content needs.

   Do some experiments (being careful not to veer too far away from your established brand style guidelines) to get a feel for the optimum topics, length and post frequency.

Interaction is a reliable gauge; likes, shares, retweets, +1s, and any other general response is good, while silence is typically a sign that something doesn't resonate. If you make a post and nothing happens (in other words, no one responds in any way), chances are something is wrong. To identify whether it's the timing or the topic that missed the mark, try another post with a different topic at the exact same time on the exact same day of the week the following week. Silence again could mean the time of day was off; a better response could mean the topic was the culprit. Learn from what you observe to get stronger more targeted content in front of the right people at the right time.

It's also important to understand how different social networks function to really get a feel for each network's etiquette and preferences. For instance, Twitter is a microblogging network that thrives on fast-paced creation and curation. It can be appropriate to post eight or more tweets throughout a single day. On the other hand, Facebook is slower paced, and you may find your followers annoyed by more than two or three Facebook posts per day. Know what you're working with before you jump in with both feet.

4) **Stay focused:** Pick content that you find interesting, but keep your selections focused on your niche. For instance, if you are a catering company, there's really no reason for your brand's Facebook page to be curating articles about the top 10 Beyoncé songs. It's okay to show different sides of your personality, but don't get too far off track subject-wise. So if your catering company's demographic is young people interested in pop culture, it might be reasonable to share an article about various celebrities' favorite foods. It's really up to each and every brand to decide for themselves the boundaries of their content curation.

SEO-Friendly Content Curation in a Post-Panda World

By Virginia Nussey

The challenge for a brand committed to supporting itself as a publisher is deciding how to scale its personnel and participation.

Exactly how brands manage content departments across their owned-media channels and off-site communities like Facebook, Twitter, blogs and groups is a new challenge to tackle in today's conversational media reality. Being a publisher requires competent standards of quality, frequency, distribution and community management.

However, small and midsized businesses aren't typically equipped to support an in-house media team. Technology that supports publishing objectives can allow for a more robust content marketing strategy. Helping businesses reach these objectives are platforms that:

- **Frequent:** Up your publishing frequency and your share of market voice.
- **Relevant:** Generate content your audience will find topically relevant and interesting.
- **Rankable:** Create content with SEO ranking potential.

An SEO Test of Curated Content

Evaluating curation from an SEO standpoint centers around the question of rankability. In the face of Google's Panda-related algorithm factors, the quality of content is of utmost importance to ranking. Panda devalues duplicate content and over-optimized content (content intended only for search engine rankings, as indicated by manipulative practices such as keyword stuffing).

"Curation" is a dirty word among some SEOs and content marketers. How can repackaging someone else's content deliver non-duplicated content to the publisher and unique value to readers? The Google Panda update was a clear signal that content must be unique and of high quality to be eligible for top rankings.

Through testing, we identified characteristics of curated content that does adhere to guidelines for quality content outlined by Google. A complete accounting of our test and results can be found in the full version of this article, which originally appeared in our "SEO Newsletter" (see the URL provided at the end of this section). Our findings showed that the same ranking potential can be gained from curated content with editorialized curation, but in significantly less time than a traditional blog post.

Guidelines for Content Curation That Meets SEO Quality Standards

- **Text should be unique** — Duplicate content offers a website no value. Google filters duplication from search results. Readers are unlikely to read duplicate content or share it with their networks. A general length guideline is 200+ unique words of editorialized content per curated story.

SEO-Friendly Content Curation in a Post-Panda World (continued)

- **Sources linked to should be of high quality** — Authorities on the web are understood to link to other authorities. External links to authority sources may be recognized by Google as a sign of useful content.

- **Add value** — Add value to the collection, such as through storytelling, a new perspective or commentary. Google's quality content guidelines expressly state: "Think about what makes your website unique, valuable, or engaging. Make your website stand out from others in your field."[3]

Take care that everything you publish on behalf of your brand serves a purpose, speaks to the audience in a voice of leadership, and ultimately provides something special to your audience. Curation need not be the straight reporting of facts. A collection can come together to weave a story or unveil an overlooked perspective. As with everything else, bring your creativity to your curation.

Brands today are looking for options to ease requirements for online publication. When done right, editorialized curation boosts a content strategy with content that's SEO-friendly, keyword rich, and allows for authority and thought leadership.

The full version of this article with test methodology and results can be viewed at *http://www.bruceclay.com/newsletter/volume112/seo-friendly-content-curation.htm*.

@VirginiaNussey is Bruce Clay, Inc.'s content manager. She has worked for the company since 2008 as a writer, blogger, industry reporter and communications strategist.

Remember the "Why" behind Curation

As marketers and business owners, we curate and create content for the same reasons — to build relationships, communicate ideas, respond to demand and actively participate in our niche communities. Curation is an incredibly powerful tool that allows us to express who we are using the words of others, and as such, it can be an incredible resource to help us get the right content in the place at the right time more quickly and more often.

But remember that with great power comes great responsibility. The content you curate represents you, so it's essential that your content be thoughtful, strategic and targeted at all times to avoid careless endorsements and PR nightmares.

Chapter Notes

[1] Kristi Kellogg, "SMX Advanced 2013 Recap: 32 Takeaways." Bruce Clay, Inc. blog. 14 June 2013. <http://www.bruceclay.com/blog/2013/06/smx-advanced-2013-recap/>

[2] Matt Cutts, "Is it useful to have a section of my site that re-posts articles from other sites?" GoogleWebmasterHelp video. 5 May 2012. <http://www.youtube.com/watch?v=o7sfUDr3w8l>

[3] "Webmaster Guidelines: Best practices to help Google find, crawl, and index your site." Google Webmaster Tools Help. Accessed 12 November 2013. <https://support.google.com/webmasters/answer/35769?hl=en>

Chapter 6

Video: It's Time to Shine

Video offers the most personal form of interaction a brand can have with customers short of being in the same room with them. That makes video powerful, but it also puts a huge responsibility in your hands as a content developer.

If video is going to be part of your content marketing campaign, you need to spend as much time on the quality of the video as you do on its content. A video has power because it's visual, and its impact will be proportional to the intentionality and production work that went into creating it.

The Advantages of Video

Videos tend to create a much more personal connection with the audience than text does. We're social beings, wired to relate better when we see a face and hear a voice. Video provides a better opportunity to let your audience get to know you than any other online format.

Some subjects just work better on video, such as explaining how to change a car tire. In addition, a portion of your audience will simply prefer to absorb information via video rather than reading text.

Of the many reasons why you should put time, energy and money into making video part of your content marketing, these stand out:

- **Personality:** Video shows personality in more dimensions than any other kind of content. Things like sentiment, earnestness and body language come through.

- **Shareability:** Most people love to be on video. Being featured makes them feel special and can give them an air of authority. As a result, people love to share video content that includes themselves.

- **Multi-Sensory Communication:** Flashy videos draw eyeballs, but quality information that involves sounds, words and action keeps people riveted. Video allows you to present information more creatively than you can with straight text or still images.

- **Syndication:** You have many opportunities to syndicate your videos across multiple channels online, which gets your content in front of a lot of people.

- **Novelty:** Everyone can create photos and text pretty well. Being able to do video well makes you stand out.

Making Videos in Various Contexts

Online video is growing up fast. What used to take an entire team of professionals to create just a few years ago is now something anyone can produce.

Video comes from all kinds of sources in all levels of quality. Some is produced out of a studio, some is shot professionally at a conference or live event, and then there are the ubiquitous smartphone videos. All three can play a role in a content marketing campaign.

Studio-Recorded Content

Studios are great for making content in a controlled environment. If you have a mostly empty room, then use it as the set. Put up a green screen for a few hundred dollars and you can make it look like anywhere (using video effects software). If you are just getting started with video production, a studio gives you a place to practice and get it right before anyone else sees your videos.

Studio settings enable you to set up controlled lighting and sound and get precisely what you are looking for. The drawback is that they can look very staged and stale. If you plan to launch a lot of video-based content, consider creating a dedicated studio environment where you can hone your skills.

> *As the interviewer, you're viewed as a thought leader; when you promote the interview, you're actually promoting someone else.*

Live-Streamed Content

Videotaping and streaming content live is an exciting form of video content. Murray has produced and hosted live shows on Justin.TV and managed YouTube celebrities doing live shows to promote products and whip up engagement. It works. People respond to live content because they can feel part of it. This applies to everything from participatory events, as you can do on **Google Hangouts** (*http://www.google.com/+/learnmore/hangouts*), all the way to live interviews or events.

Putting together a live show is challenging. You only have that one chance to bring everything together and deliver it in a compelling way. On the plus side, the broadcast can be very interactive. If you get fan engagement, they can interact live on social media as a group. This is taking a bit of a risk because you never know what people are going to do or say, but the community engagement may be worth the risk.

For example, Murray worked with YouTube celebrity JaackMaate to promote a video platform and asked him to get his fans to tweet answers. JaackMaate has a large fan base that he can engage with to promote companies and products that are applicable to his audience, which is predominantly teenage girls in the UK. In a live-streamed video show, he asked his fans questions live and had them post answers on his fan page or through tweets on Twitter. The result: He received 5,000 tweets in an hour, making his hashtag trend nationally in the UK. In this way, he was able to get his fans to interact with the company's product in real time and gain momentum on social media.

Interviews as Content

Interviews make phenomenal content because they are inherently a partnership. As the interviewer, you have advantages. You're viewed as a thought leader because you are creating the content, and when you promote that interview you are actually promoting someone else. At the same time, the person you interview will most likely share that content with his or her own social network — and that helps promote your brand, as well.

> *If you want to reach out to others in your industry, asking for an interview is a great way to make connections.*

Murray has conducted hundreds of interviews for Performance Marketing Insider (see *http://www.youtube.com/user/TheMailDotCom1* for current links) and other sites. The approach to these video interviews aligns with the storytelling focus we have been talking about throughout this book: you tell your story and build your personal brand through the content you produce. Interviews function as an important part of Murray's own content marketing strategy.

Industry events offer amazing opportunities for this type of content, especially if you shoot interviews (as shown in Figure 6-1). At conferences, you are able to choose interviewees from a potential pool of thousands, and you have the opportunity to shoot lots of interviews in a short space of time. Murray has shot as many as 100 interviews in three days. That meant working from 9 a.m. to 3 a.m. the next morning for three days in a row; it's crazy, but it can be done.

Figure 6-1: Co-authors Murray and Bruce record an interview at a conference.

Another way to shoot interviews is over Skype. You can reach people all around the world and get experts to weigh in on various topics. Skype often makes it much easier to interview people even when they're local, since they can be more relaxed in their own environment.

However you create them, video interviews can have a wide reach. They may even draw a global audience. While traveling in China, for instance, Murray had many people come up to him who had watched his videos and were fans of the show.

How to Create Great Interview Content

Here are some tips, learned through experience, for making your video interviews the best they can be:

- **Plan a topic:** It's a good idea to interview people about a specific topic rather than just start talking to them and waiting to see what happens. People online usually search for a topic, a person or a company, so focus your interviews.

- **Pick interesting people:** Work hard to find interesting people who can say something stimulating about a popular topic. An interviewee may give insights that educate viewers; then viewers may want to share the interview. It is a bonus if your interview subjects are well-known and can promote your content to a larger audience themselves.

- **Help the interviewee relax:** You want the people you interview to feel relaxed and comfortable in the situation so they will perform well on camera. Most of the people Murray interviews aren't full-time spokespeople. They have probably given only a few interviews before. A big part of his role as interviewer is to set the person up for success so that he will get the best interview possible, both in terms of content and making the person look good.

- **Talk about it first:** Discuss what you could talk about in the interview before rolling tape. Once you have discussed it with the interviewee, talk them through how the interview will work. Together you can briefly discuss the questions and the answers that they might give. A good tip is to tell them that if the interview does not work, we can always reshoot it. Nine times out of ten a second shoot isn't necessary, but knowing that it's an option takes the pressure off.

Conducting interviews provides many personal branding advantages. By being on camera so much and having so many viewers for his videos, Murray has become well known in his industry. If you want to reach out to others in your industry, asking for an interview is a great way to make connections. It can open many doors.

Six Tips to Help You Get Started Creating Great Video Consistently

By Alyce Currier

Just like blogging, video isn't something you should do once and then be done with. To make it work, you need to figure out how to make video over and over again. We understand that making video can be intimidating (especially making lots of video), so here are six tips for getting started:

1) Make five videos, not one.

Don't start with your front page video! Instead, address some smaller friction points with video so you can experiment with lower-pressure content. For example, answer a support question that you get all the time, or make a video to accompany a blog post.

2) Remove creative barriers.

Placing constraints on yourself means you don't have to make big decisions about every video, every time. For example, every Whiteboard Friday that Moz publishes takes the same format: a Moz-er or a featured guest standing in front of a whiteboard. Removing creative decisions makes it easier to focus on the content!

3) Routine scheduling.

If you're having trouble making video a habit, think about starting a low-pressure weekly series that you can commit to. Keep a master list of content ideas so you always have a topic to attack.

4) Start simple with production.

If you don't have expensive video equipment, don't worry! Luckily, your message is more important than a high-budget production. You can shoot totally acceptable videos with a smartphone, a repurposed conference room, and a few lights placed around your face to even out shadows.

5) Be human.

One of video's biggest superpowers is its ability to scale communication in a way that feels personal and human, so think of every video you make as an opportunity to be more human. Put a human bumper on a webinar. Shoot a culture video capturing your company's personality. Keep your script conversational if you can.

6) Freely share your knowledge and expertise.

One of the most effective ways to use video to build trust is to share your knowledge. Video is a great way to make information more memorable, fun, and shareable, so try adding it to your content marketing efforts!

Alyce Currier is the content strategist at Wistia. Contact her on Twitter @NotAlyce or find more video production, marketing, and concepting tips in the Wistia Learning Center at *http://wistia.com/learning*.

Using Videos to Create Brand Awareness

Example 1: Blendtec

Probably the most frequently cited case study about corporate videos is Blendtec's "Will it Blend?" campaign (*http://www.willitblend.com*), a series of videos in which the company uses its product to blend popular items, from tiki torches to smartphones, and show what happens (see Figure 6-2).

Hundreds of millions of views later, Blendtec has seen its sales figures skyrocket and has become a cultural touch point. Understanding the typical YouTube viewer, they built content demonstrating what everyone has always wanted to do with a blender, but would never dare to do at home. The campaign worked because it was fun, and it showed the product benefits in an engaging context.

Figure 6-2: *The Will It Blend? videos exemplify brilliant content marketing. (Photo courtesy of Blendtec.com)*

Example 2: Brian Solis TV

One of the best known business-to-business video content marketers is Brian Solis, who has used his popular video series talking about the impact of technology, culture and business (*http://www.youtube.com/user/BrianSolisTV*) to build his own brand. He talked to us about how he got started.

Solis said that having been behind the camera as a photographer for a long time, he really did not like being on camera. However, he began making videos because he realized they would be great solid content for the kinds of topics he wanted to be found for. If anyone was looking for these topics, he wanted to show up in their research. His video strategy worked, and today he is one of the most sought-after speakers and consultants on marketing topics in the country.

Targeting Video at Search

Video marketing is a vast subject that could easily merit its own publication. Here we'll give you a high-level introduction to video optimization; we hope you'll use it as a jumping off point to understanding what search engines take into consideration to determine where your videos rank in the search engine results pages (SERPs).

Since high-quality video content takes time and resources to

Earning likes and comments on YouTube videos isn't just about building brand loyalty and community. It also influences ranking.

produce, it's crucial that your videos are indexed by search engines. Then they can be put in front of the right people at the right time — when they're searching for what your video offers.

Connecting Brands and YouTube Stars

By Jordan Armstrong

I was fortunate to help identify a new type of marketing back in 2007/2008, when I worked with BeautyChoice.com. The company was struggling to sell beauty items online, and we were searching for a better way. At the time, the company was spending a ton of money online in areas such as AdWords, PPC and SEO. We needed to think outside the box in order to save the company. Simply, put we needed a new way to sell product!

One evening, I saw my then-girlfriend using her flat iron as a curling iron. I thought that was odd, but it sparked my attention. I then thought, if she was weird, maybe there are others just like her. I decided to go to YouTube and type in: "How to curl your hair with a flat iron." That is when the magic light bulb turned on.

There were several videos (in 2007/08) of regular girls talking about beauty products: how to use them, where to buy them, and tips/demos. I immediately thought this was a great opportunity—maybe our company could reach out to these video publishers/beauty gurus and see if they would review our products for free in exchange for content and links back to our ecommerce store. At this time, no other company was turning to YouTube for product placement, custom content marketing, etc.

We started reaching out to more and more girls who specialized in these types of videos and started locking down contracts with them. Their job was to creatively keep doing what they were doing, but using products that made sense (provided by us) throughout their YouTube videos. BeautyChoice sponsored tons of these gurus and led the way in this type of marketing. We saw immediate success. It wasn't too long before other companies caught on to what we were doing, and the beauty stars soon realized just how valuable they were/are today.

Figure 6-3: Brand messages occasionally appear in this video by Michelle Phan, which has 34 million+ views on YouTube.[1]

Connecting Brands and YouTube Stars (continued)

Being part of BeautyChoice's pioneering effort was a great experience for me. Since then I've been fortunate to see YouTube's evolution, develop and manage YouTube stars, connect YouTubers and brands, consult for networks on YouTube, and forecast YouTube trends.

How Brands can Work with Video Publishers — I'm extremely passionate about seeing what the YouTubers are doing and how companies can work with them. Overall, they need each other in order for this type of marketing to continue to work.

But companies and content creators/video publishers must work together in the right way. It's the company's job to creatively seek opportunities for YouTubers. It's the YouTube publisher's job to consistently create authentic and engaging content for their viewers. YouTubers who focus on working with the right companies and who stay open-minded about new opportunities always set new trends.

Top Pointers — If you have a brand looking to increase its success in this type of marketing/advertising, keep these tips in mind:

- *Right fit:*
  Work with the right influencer(s) in your vertical. Focus on your marketing and identifying those YouTubers.

- *Calls to action:*
  The sweeter the deal, most of the time the greater the results. These YouTubers want to make sure their subscribers/fans are being taken care of. They love hosting/running things like contests, promotions, exclusive offerings, giveaways, and spotlights.

- *Celebrity inspired:*
  We would closely watch what celebrities were in the news and have the YouTuber use that for ideas/inspiration.

- *Shock effect:*
  Create shocking, out-of-the-box content. The more shocking your videos are, the more attention they get.

- *Authenticity:*
  Make sure the content is not too commercial or it will come across like it's scripted. The more authentic the video is, the more likely users will watch and act.

- *Don't force products:*
  If a YouTube star doesn't like a product, accept it gracefully. You will count your blessings. The audience can tell if a YouTuber really likes a product/service/company or not.

Jordan Armstrong is a YouTube strategy expert, marketing consultant, and entrepreneur located in Scottsdale, AZ. Contact info: @YotaCast

SEO Factors for Video

Not all videos are created equal in the eyes of search engines. To earn a spot at the top of the SERPs in front of the right market, you need to remember four main factors:

- Quality, content and engagement matter.

- Keyword research is important.

- Google reads words, and it's important to put those words in the right places.

- Adding video Sitemaps can improve your video's SERP rank and presentation.

1) Quality Matters

We'll say it again: quality matters! Before you start trying to think like a search engine, it's critical to remember that *people* are your target market. For better or worse, the video content you publish inevitably represents your brand. It should go without saying that you want your brand to be represented by high-quality, benefit-driven video content that is engaging, helpful and worthy of your viewer's time, likes, comments and shares.

Both YouTube and Google take into account how users interact with your video content to gauge community interest, brand authority, relevance and — ultimately — rank in search results. This means earning likes and comments on your YouTube videos isn't just about building brand loyalty and community. It also influences ranking. If you're interested in seeing top-three results, creating content that inspires engagement is critical.

What you *say* in your video can also impact your video's SERP rank. Google (and YouTube, which is owned by Google) actually references video transcripts and captions to understand the content. A spoken keyword phrase near the beginning of your video can go a long way in helping Google to identify your content as the most relevant solution to a search query, so taking time to plan and write scripts should be considered a critical component of video optimization.

2) Keyword Research Is Important

As with any other content, video optimization starts with keyword research. It boils down to figuring out what your target market is asking for, and how they are asking for it, so you can create content that addresses the requests.

> *Syndicating a video can pay off by exponentially multiplying your view counts.*

When you're thinking about keyword phrases and content strategy, remember that informational videos (and accordingly informational keywords like "how to do XYZ") will generally get you better engagement and search rankings than transactional-style videos (with transaction-geared keywords like "buy XYZ") that are focused on product placement and hard sells.

The same keyword research and audience targeting principles apply that we've discussed earlier (see Chapter 2), but there is a specialized tool you can use for video research. YouTube has its own keyword tool to tell you what people are looking for: *https://ads.youtube.com/keyword_tool*

3) Put Your Keywords Where Google Can Find Them

Since search spiders can't watch your video, they glean relevance based on the words in your video's transcript, Meta information, captions, surrounding text and the HTML associated with your video.

This is where your keyword research comes into play. Keywords should be placed (but not stuffed) in the following places:

- **Video Title, Description:** Make sure to use your keyword phrase early on in your Titles and Descriptions.

- **File name:** What you name your video file can also include a keyword, such as *how-to-change-a-tire.mov*.

- **Audio script:** Remember to *say* your keyword out loud in your movie so that it becomes a part of the transcript or captions file associated with your video. Strategically writing a script will be an invaluable addition to your content creation process.

- **Landing page:** Upload your video to YouTube.com, but, when appropriate, also create a landing page for your video on your website. Embed your video on the landing page, and then add text that describes or supplements the video, as well as still images. Diverse, rich-media landing pages are engaging, offer a strong user experience and give Google a lot of context that helps your website's ranking improve along with your individual YouTube (or Vimeo or other) video's ranking.

- **Tags on the landing page:** If your video is embedded into a landing page on your website, make sure to use the same keyword phrase in the landing page HTML in the Title and Meta Description tags.

4) Create a Video Sitemap

Video Sitemaps can improve your video's rank and SERP presentation. If you embed a YouTube or Vimeo video onto your website, creating and submitting a Sitemap for that video will make it easier for search engines to find and index your embedded video. This includes increased representation in Google video searches.

Video Sitemaps can also be used to add a thumbnail image and an optimized title to your video's SERP result, even in regular web searches. Along with improving the opportunity for a higher rank, these Sitemap additions make your video SERP result stand out from the crowd which can significantly improve engagement and click-through (as shown in Figure 6-4).

Cooking Artichokes - How to Cook Artichokes Video
video.about.com/italianfood/**Artichokes**.htm ▾
Apr 12, 2007
Artichokes are fun to eat and taste great in **recipes**. Watch three
easy ways to **cook** an **artichoke**, plus ...

Figure 6-4: A video search result can include an image, which increases clicks.

Creating a video Sitemap is something that even novices can do
using the YouTube or Vimeo embed code (make sure you're using
the "old" <object> version of the code), any number of video
Sitemap generators or Google Webmaster Tools.

TIPS: *For details on creating a video Sitemap, see Google Help at*
https://support.google.com/webmasters/answer/80472?h
l=en.
For more video SEO tips, go to
http://www.bruceclay.com/blog/2013/06/10-video-seo-
tips-to-improve-serp-rank

Promoting Videos

Once you've created video content, how can you get maximum
value from it? Beyond uploading it to YouTube and embedding it on
your site, you'll want to promote your video.

Using Syndication for Greater Exposure

Understandably, YouTube gives popular videos more prominence.
So if you can get some momentum on one of your videos, it will
help your ranking with video searches. This is where syndication
can pay off by exponentially multiplying your view counts.

A corporate client once hired Murray to develop publicity for their
product. He decided to make a video series about the product and
its uses. He pitched to a number of publications that he would make
the video series, and many of them agreed to carry the videos. At
the end of each video, the logos of all the publications appeared as
"Media Partners" (see Figure 6-5). Murray also wrote unique text
(not duplicated) that each publication could easily post on their site

along with the embedded videos.

The overall effect of this was that every publication carried the series of 10 videos with the unique text content he had provided for each site. The video series received lots of exposure for the client, and the publications liked carrying the videos because they offered original content for their readers. This was a great exchange for all concerned.

Figure 6-5: Syndication partners can help distribute your video to a wider audience.

Integrating Video with Blogs

Writing a blog article about a video is another way to promote it. Videos are easy to embed into blog posts and can supplement the text. This means that you can get exposure for a blog post, optimized to bring in traffic, and that traffic will also benefit the view numbers on your video content.

A video's view counts can be fickle when it's embedded in a blog post, though. Even if the post with the embedded video gets lots of shares, the number of people who share the post compared to the number of people who watch the video can be 10 to 1. Meaning that for every 10 people who see or even share the post, only one of them will watch the video.

Thus, there's a strong case for promoting the video on its own through YouTube and other channels. Creating video strictly as a way to enhance the content in a blog post itself is an approach unto itself, but for maximum exposure you'll both upload the video to a video search engine and embed it within relevant content on your blog or website.

> *Focus on quality over quantity in everything you do—from content writing and strategy to video.*

Lights, Camera, *Action!*

Whether you are creating polished video in a studio, generating interviews and live content at an event, or encouraging and re-sharing video from your fans and customers, video is a powerful way to tell your brand story and make a content marketing campaign both personal and memorable.

Remember to stay focused on quality over quantity in everything you do — from content writing and strategy to video shooting and optimization. Think of every video as your one chance to catch people's attention, make a connection and represent your brand the way you want it to be remembered.

Think outside the box about how a video can physically show your audience something that will help them better remember your brand and what you do. Don't miss your opportunity to make an impression by publishing bland video content that doesn't resonate with the right demographic.

Be thoughtful about your content and proud of what you publish. Create something catchy and it will catch on.

Chapter Notes

[1] Michelle Phan, "Lady GaGa Poker Face Tutorial." YouTube video uploaded May 8, 2009. <http://www.youtube.com/watch?v=YFMaLuI1uxc>

Chapter 7

Images: It's About the Message

We are visual creatures, and the web is becoming increasingly visual. A picture is truly worth a thousand words; a collection of photos taken on mobile phones is worth a billion dollars. At least that's what Facebook CEO Mark Zuckerberg thought when he bought Instagram.

The Power of Images

Photos have always been an important part of an online presence, but over the last five years they have become a focal point. Social media has elevated the sharing of photos, and today there are millions of photos uploaded to the Internet every day. The most popular blogs that write about fashion, celebrities or sports make heavy use of images, to the great benefit of their traffic. In kind, many of the rising social media networks, like Tumblr, Instagram and Pinterest, are all based around images.

In 2010 it became clear how much Facebook values images when the social network raised its maximum image size to 2048 pixels — an eight-fold increase over the previous maximum size. Facebook today doesn't even specify dimensions, just a generous 25MB file size limit.[1] Further, the site's redesign in spring 2013 was marked by its emphasis on images, making them larger in the News Feed and allowing feeds to be sorted by categories, including photos only.

The emphasis on images makes sense. Since an overwhelming amount of content exists out there, it is easy for people to skim over text. With a photo, all you have to do is skim — that's how you look at images! One great shot from an event can tell the whole story that you want people to take away. One funny picture in your feed can do wonders to humanize your company's image.

Anyone with a phone can take a photo and quickly upload it to social media. Does that make it good content marketing? No, but it does go to show how comfortable people are taking and sharing photos as part of their social lives. You can capitalize on that by using photos in your campaigns. Create and share photos that will draw people in, get shared and drive people to take the next step down the sales funnel. That's good content marketing.

Why Photos Help with Content Marketing

Photos drive a ton of sharing. Dan Zarella did a fantastic study over at HubSpot where he created and analyzed a database of more than 1.3 million posts from the top 10,000 most-liked Facebook pages. He found that photos get liked and shared much more frequently than text, video or other kinds of posts.[2]

Pinterest and sites like it that are built around images and image sharing are statistically proven to lead directly to sales. A study by Bizrate Insights found that:

 32% of online buyers in North America have made a purchase as a result of seeing an image on a social image-sharing site, such as Pinterest."

– eMarketer.com[3]

Whatever your content marketing objectives, whether you want more social media exposure or increased sales, photos will help.

How a Fashion Gig Got Me Started with Image Marketing

By Trent Partridge

I started working as an SEO about the same time I started working as a photographer. I left Rooms To Go, where I had been a successful salesman, applied for a job at the bottom of an Internet marketing company, was hired, and bought a Nikon camera the morning I started my new job.

As my Internet marketing skills got better, so did my photography. In fact, the day I got certified in SEO from the University of Southern Mississippi was the day I got my first good-paying gig as a fashion photographer for a show in South Beach.

The photos I took turned out well (see below). Afterwards I remember one of the show organizers saying, "We need to get these pictures up quick and I need them to be seen by lots of people. Not just by people who visit our website but on other websites."

It was that sentence that ended up being my gateway into the world of image content marketing spliced with search engine optimization (SEO) — or, what I simply call "image marketing" today.

5 Steps that Helped Make the South Beach Fashion Show an Image Marketing Success

The South Beach fashion show image campaign was a success. Overall the organizers saw 23% of visits coming from image search, 10% from external links, and the gain of two power clients who said they found the organizers either through image search or an external link.

Here are the five steps I took to make the South Beach fashion show an image marketing success.

How a Fashion Gig Got Me Started with Image Marketing (continued)

1) Renamed Images, Taking Care to Include Keyword Phrases

After I dumped my images to my computer, the first thing I did was change the image names to include keywords. So, for the South Beach fashion show I changed the file names from something that looked like this:

- Nikon - DSC_001.JPG
- Nikon - IMG.2813.RAW

to this:

- South-Beach-fashion-show-Armani.jpg
- South-Beach-fashion-show-models.jpg

2) Increased Image Visibility by Posting to Social Sites

With the images renamed, I posted from 5 to 50 show images onto Flickr, Photobucket and StumbleUpon and linked each of the images back to the fashion organizer's website. The result was a great gain in views on the social sites, and extra traffic to the organizer's website because of the included backlinks.

3) Linked to Images from Optimized Blog Posts and Web Content

I optimized blog and article recaps of the South Beach fashion show by including keyword-rich links from the content back to the images. This tactic is great for image search optimization as well as viral article marketing.

4) Turned Images into Videos Linked to the Organizer's Website

Converting images to video is a great content marketing strategy.

To apply this technique to the Miami fashion photos, I created a slideshow with 20 images, converted the slideshow to video, and added links back to the fashion organizer's website in a closing frame of the video, as well as the video's description. The video gained great views and traffic back to the website.

5) Made Sure to Optimize Web Pages with Image ALT Attributes

My final step was to re-optimize the fashion organizer's website for the keyword phrase [south beach fashion shows]. Using standard SEO methodology, I included the phrase in the Meta Description, link anchor text and image ALT attributes.

Trent Partridge is the author of *Internet Marketing For Music Artists, Models and Entertainers, MyPropFolio Social Media Workbook*, and contributing writer for *Be a Real Estate Heavyweight*. He is also a photographer, basketball speed and agility trainer, foster parent, and co-founder of nonprofit Wanna Help and Sketch Comic.

Social Media's Impact on Photo Sharing

Great content marketing photos tell a story, have a message and compel people to take action.

Any photo that is part of your content marketing should do a little of each. One thing to avoid is sharing photos just because you can. A single exciting image can make a big impact, but even a powerful image can get lost in a sea of mediocre ones.

Let's look at the introduction of Flickr, Facebook and Instagram onto the Internet scene over the years to get an idea of the growing role that photos are playing as the Internet evolves. We'll discuss how you can take advantage of these three platforms, each of which has built a wildly successful site around photos and photo sharing.

Phase 1: Flickr

Flickr opened its virtual doors in 2004 and was acquired by Yahoo! in 2005. It quickly grew to become the largest photo site on the web. Flickr's proposition was simple and, at the time, amazing: anyone taking pictures could simply upload them, tag them and have an online repository of all of their photography. Today the site is still a key tool for photographers and bloggers to host images, but its popularity has waned (see Figure 7-1).

Images you host on Flickr get cached and indexed by the search engines, so they may show up in search results.

Why has it lost popularity? Because there's *no story*. Flickr is a place to store photos. But there's no inherent way for users to tie photos together, other than basic photo-set organization and the fact that they are taken by the same person.

Figure 7-1: Flickr provides image storage with SEO benefits.

Using a Flickr Account to Boost My SEO

So we've established that, for all intents and purposes, Flickr is an online repository for photography. While it doesn't have any of the glitz, glam or longevity of more interactive social media sites like Facebook, that doesn't mean that adding photos to Flickr isn't a marketing opportunity, especially if one of your main goals is to get your photos seen.

Flickr can do three things for your brand that will help with your SEO efforts either directly or indirectly:

1) **Indexing benefit:** Images you host on Flickr get cached and indexed by the search engines, so they may show up in search results. To get the most out of this benefit, make sure to perform keyword research and pick keywords you would like your images to rank for. Then include your keywords naturally in your photo sets and collections, set and collection descriptions, image titles, image descriptions and image file names. This can directly help your SEO by making your images show up in image searches more often and higher up (if the optimization is done well).

2) **Traffic benefit:** Flickr allows you to put links in your image

and subset descriptions that go to your website. While all links from Flickr are automatically tagged `rel="nofollow"` (which means they won't help your link authority), they *will* help drive traffic to your site. This can increase popularity and social media sharing.

3) **Links benefit:** Although the actual links you add to your Flickr descriptions won't count as inbound links for SEO, the wide reach that Flick photo storage gives you might actually help your web pages gain inbound links in a more indirect way. As mentioned, Flickr can help get your images placed in image search results; then if other businesses (that are related to your subject matter) approach you to use your image on their website, ask them to link to a relevant page on your website from the article or web page housing the image. And, *voila*! We have link building.

Phase 2: Facebook

Facebook started out in 2004 as a website for college students to connect, with photo sharing being a key feature of the network. By 2009, Facebook was reigning as the most-used social network in the world. The key to its rise was enabling users to share photos with their friends. As the site evolved, people learned to upload photos that their friends would "like," and the social site's popularity grew accordingly.

> *By attaching interesting, on-topic imagery to your Facebook posts, you're building your brand and . . . helping to drive traffic and conversions.*

The types of photos people share are telling. We like to share scenes from vacations, holidays and important life events because those are key moments of our individual stories.

When brands got into Facebook, the same thing happened. You don't see many pictures of a business' storefront or office building in the timelines of brand pages. Instead, what you see are photos of the brand being integrated into peoples' lives, or of the brand changing and growing over time. You see photos that *tell the story of the brand*.

Since 2009, Facebook itself has evolved a lot, including the 2012 addition of the Timeline feature, which now seems forehead-slappingly commonplace. Of course people want to organize the photos they take in chronological order! That's how we live, and that's how stories are told.

What You Need to Know about Optimizing for Facebook

First things first: Facebook content is *not* currently indexed by search engines (though this could change). So the physical act of placing optimized images or words on your Facebook page is not going to help increase the rank of your web pages in the search engine results pages (SERPs).

That said, you can still use Facebook as an invaluable asset to drive traffic and sales, establish relationships with your customers and prospective customers, and nurture brand loyalty. (See Chapter 9 for more on the benefits of social media marketing with Facebook.)

It's about the message the photo is sending, not just the photo itself.

But if you can't optimize images for search with Facebook, why are we talking about it? Well, Facebook has its own algorithm for determining which of your Facebook posts actually land in the News Feeds of your followers (also known as the people who have "liked" your brand page).

Yes, that's right. Not everyone who likes your page automatically sees your Facebook updates in their personal News Feed.

Here's how it all ties together. A Facebook post launched with an image attached sees significantly more shares, likes, and comments than a text-only post, and one of the main algorithmic factors is engagement volume. So, by attaching interesting, on-topic imagery to your Facebook posts, you're not only building your brand and keeping your content marketing top notch, you're also helping to drive traffic and conversions by getting your content in front of the right people at the right time.

Phase 3: Instagram, Pinterest, etc.

Now, Instagram and Pinterest are quickly growing and have built their user-base specifically by letting people share photo content in unique ways.

Figure 7-1: *Instagram lets users easily apply filters to photos. (Photo credit: Instagram.com blog)*

Instagram uses a chronological timeline, but differentiates itself from Facebook by allowing users to add personality to photos using filters.

Pinterest eschews the timeline format, opting instead for a topical grouping. Essentially this format has made Pinterest a host for anyone who wants to group photos around a niche interest. Another distinction is that photos need not be taken by the account holder, and in fact, most aren't. A Pinterest board is a lot like a mood board or a brainstorming session, where people "pin" photos from around the web that are tied together by common visual elements or a core topic. And it works. People are able to tell stories about themselves through boards by combining what they like into a group.

Brands can learn a lot from each of these photo sharing social networks, but if there can be only one takeaway, this should be it:

people like photos, and people like photos more when they are presented in a way that tells a story. And people take action because of photos that tell that story creatively around an interest or niche topic.

These are each important lessons for brands that want to use photos for content marketing. It's about the message the photo is sending, not just the photo itself. It's even more about the collective message over time that shows the brand personality, ideally around a niche topic.

Integrating Images into Content Marketing

Photos and other images can integrate with your content marketing campaign in many ways. Because they tell such a powerful story without using any words, it's important to choose what photos you share carefully. And remember that they need to be tied to business objectives, not just shared willy-nilly.

Posting your brand photos can expand brand awareness, link people back to your website or sales pages, and build relationships, especially if you curate photos from fans and colleagues.

What to Consider before Sharing a Photo

Here are some questions to think about before using photos as part of your content marketing campaign:

- Why are you sharing the photo? How does it support your overall objectives?

- What do you want people to do when they see the photo?

- What story are you telling with your photo? How do you want people to feel about your brand, and does this photo encourage that?

- Are there people in it? Viewers tend to be drawn to pictures with people in them.

- Does the photo communicate clearly what it is? Is it a quality image with good contrast? Eye-tracking studies show that people look most often at images that have high contrast between the subject and background, and a clearly discernible subject.[3]

- Will it be easy for someone who sees it to share it to their network? Share buttons make this easy (see Figure 7-2).

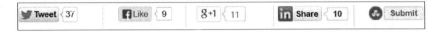

Figure 7-2: Share buttons on your pages facilitate sharing your content.

How Photos Can Help Tell a Story

Photos work best when they work in conjunction with some kind of related text or show a person doing something. This is especially true with pictures taken at live events. But the success of photos at live events has a lot to do with the fact that we, as humans, like to see people in the photos we look at.

Everything from car ads to street team marketing banks on the fact that people are more likely to have a positive impression of a product if there is a person alongside it. Any good television commercial is going to have people using the product being sold. Similarly, if you are a consulting agency and your "product" is providing strategy, your marketing efforts will bring in more customers by showing hard-working people having fun alongside your latest report than by showing the report alone. We react to people and faces.

> *The best subjects are faces smiling, or people or things in action that capture a sense of the moment.*

Here are some key ways photos can help you tell your brand story:

- Show people using your product.

- Expand on what you're talking about with other paid and text campaigns.

- Help people visualize your messaging.

- Increase brand awareness if you add your company's watermark or logo.

- Show your social side by picturing live events, office parties or other.

Taking Photos at Events

Photos are an excellent way of extending the reach of a live event. For one, attendees naturally take photos and upload them online. Also, people respond to photos of themselves on social media by sharing them, thus extending the reach of your event. These facts create a huge opportunity for you to encourage photo-taking as part of spreading a particular message at an event you either host or attend.

One way is to **create photos by hiring a photographer** or designating one from within your organization. You'll create a mountain of content that you can share after the event, or curate content to emphasize specific aspects of your event. Sometimes it's better to share a handful of amazing shots rather than hundreds, but it's always nice to have those hundreds to choose from.

Another way is to **give people a reason to share their own photos**. For example, Ford Motor Company created a content marketing promotion for the new Escape at an event. They set up a special photo booth where people could get their picture taken with Scott Monty, Ford's head of social media. Ford put its branding on the photos in the hopes that these would be shared. This photo booth was a simple but effective way of creating content that people wanted to share (see Figure 7-1).

Figure 7-1: Murray Newlands with Scott Monty, taken in an event photo booth.

Being the Photographer

Being the photographer at events is fantastic. Here's why.

Whether at an event, show or party, people love having their picture taken. When Murray straps on a camera, he typically takes up to 500 photos in an evening, anticipating that 30 to 50 will come out well.

What makes a good photo? The best subjects are faces smiling at the camera, or people or things in action that capture a sense of the moment.

> *Taking photos of people who you know are heavy social media users will increase the chances that those images will get shared.*

Having a great camera helps, but it's not everything. The photographer and the subjects make a great photo. As a photographer, you often put much of yourself in the pictures you take. What you choose to photograph reveals a lot about you; it tells as much of a story as what is happening in the photo.

Having the confidence to go up to people, ask them to take a photo and put them in the right frame of mind to smile and pose is a large part of the role you play. It's important to ask permission when you can. Sometimes it is not appropriate to ask, but suddenly there is the chance, and you snap away.

Crowdsourcing for Photos

Another way to integrate photos into your content marketing is to ask fans and customers to take them.

For example, Coca Cola has an amazing brand with a huge social media presence. They also have real brand devotees, as evidenced by the company's ongoing photo interaction with its fans.

If you take a great photo of a Coca Cola product, post it on Facebook, and tag the brand, they will "like" it and maybe even share it on their social media presence. This rewards people for taking photos of Coca Cola products by giving them publicity; it also gives Coca Cola an endless stream of social media content that gets shared all over Facebook. This is a truly great content marketing technique achieved through photos.

How to Promote Photo Sharing

Having photos means you have created a great *social object* that people will remember. If you try posting photos from your next event, you will be surprised at the number of new social contacts you will make and how far those images will travel.

If you take great photos of people that capture them in a good light, then post them in social media and tag the individuals, those people are likely to accept the tag and share the photos on their profiles. If their friends see the photos, they will like and comment and possibly share them, too.

Specifically taking photos of people who you know are heavy social media users will increase the chances that those images will get shared out farther and wider. When you share photos on Facebook after an event, it's perfectly acceptable to add an explicit request to tag others who were at the event.

Where possible, always brand your photos with a logo or watermark and link them back to your site. This enables people to know who made them and follow the social object back to your social presence online (see Figure 7-2).

Figure 7-2: This photo taken at an event has branding in the upper-right corner. (Pictured: Murray with Elisabeth Osmeloski of Search Engine Land and Marketing Land.)

Tips for Posting Photos

Here are some key tips to optimize the impact of your event photos:

- **Be timely:** Post your event photos on Facebook during or just after the event rather than days or weeks later. Capitalize on the excitement that lingers after an event.

- **Tag key people:** Take a photo of the event organizer and tag him or her. This will help people find your photos.

- **Share group photos:** Group photos work great because when one person gets tagged, their friends find it.

- **Make good photos:** If you make someone look great, that person will promote your photos. Taking great shots is only part of the route to making great photos. The best photos often result from a lot of cleanup in Photoshop. You can do a lot to improve a good photo by balancing the light, color and sharpness, or by cropping out unwanted elements.

We mention this because even if the lighting or background isn't perfect for taking photos, it's still wise to snap a shot when and where you can. You only have one chance to capture the moment, but you have plenty of time later to polish the digital photo.

How Images Enhance Blog Posts

Adding images to a blog post helps to engage a reader by adding a visual element and thus another opportunity to connect with the reader. Images also help authors to illustrate and emphasize points made in the text. And third, they can increase the overall SEO value of a blog post.

Users generally don't stay on a web page for more than a few seconds unless their interest is immediately piqued by a clear value proposition. Adding images to blog posts is a great way to pique people's interest and hook them with an at-a-glance idea of what your content has to offer.

Once you have them hooked, images can help keep readers engaged by periodically breaking up text in longer articles, or by offering visual cues at section breaks. Images can also help tell the story itself. Remember, great photos tell stories. An image embedded in a blog post can help clarify and add to story elements. Or think how valuable an infographic can be by visually representing complex subjects.

Three Tips for Optimizing Blog Images

To get full benefit out of your blog images, here are a few technical points that will help you on the SEO front.

1) **ALT attributes:** Every image should have an ALT attribute.

While ALT attributes should be written naturally and concisely, with their main intention being to convey to search robots and visually impaired readers what the image shows, there is major SERP-position benefit to be gained from subtly working keyword phrases into ALT attributes. Never skip this step.

2) **Site speed:** Site speed is an important part of the Google algorithm, as well as overall user experience. To keep your site running quickly, ranking high and converting, try to keep images at 70KB in size or smaller so they load quickly.

3) **OpenGraph tags:** If you have social sharing buttons on your web pages and in your blog articles, add OpenGraph tags to the HTML of your web pages so that Facebook will include your blog image(s) when people click your Share, Recommend or Like buttons (see Figure 7-3).

Figure 7-3: OpenGraph tags enable an image to be shown when a user shares your post on Facebook.

Remember, social posts with images get significantly more engagement, which means more eyes on your post and more traffic to your website. Here's a brief rundown of the three most important OpenGraph tags for blog content and how to use them.

OpenGraph Tags

og:image

Purpose	Example	Requirements
This tag tells Facebook which image to show beside your OpenGraph content description when your article or web page is shared.	`<meta property="og:ima ge" content= "http://www.bruc eclay.com/blog/ filename.jpg"/>`	Images must be at least 50 x 50 pixels and not larger than 5MB in size.

og:title

Purpose	Example	Requirements
This tag specifies the headline that introduces your content in Facebook News Feeds. You can approach writing this tag as you would a Title tag.	`<meta property="og:tit le" content="10 Video SEO Tips to Improve Rank and User Experience"/>`	Title text can be up to 95 characters.

og:description

Purpose	Example	Requirements
This tag lets you describe your post (similar to what you might include in a Meta Description). This tag won't be indexed so it doesn't matter if it's keyword-rich, but it should be accurate and compelling.	`<meta property="og: description" content="This quick-read guide will help you improve your video SEO efforts in 10 steps."/>`	Description text can be up to 297 characters.

How to Make Images Go Viral

At this point you understand that strong images are social assets that can generate shares, likes and opportunities to connect with readers. But images can also be looked at as SERP rank-boosting tools. To explain how engaging images help improve search engine rankings, we have to go back to basics to recall what search engines base rank on.

Why Having Something Everyone Wants Helps My Ranking

When a user types in a search query, the search engine's number one goal is to return results that are high-quality, relevant and able to best give the user what they want. Google scans the Internet to collect clues that help them determine what web pages are about and whether the page qualifies to be in the top 10 for a specific search query.

Remember, images can help keep readers engaged by periodically breaking up text in longer articles, or by offering visual cues.

One factor Google looks at when considering the quality and relevance of your page is its inbound links. The number of pages that link to your content, the quality of these external pages and their relevance to your subject are factors Google uses when determining ranking (using a measure called *PageRank*).

If you create an image that people like so much that they link to it, you've got yourself a *link magnet*. If there are thousands of high-quality websites linking to your image, for example a viral infographic, Google sees this as a signal that the web page housing your image is both high-quality and very important to a lot of people, which signals to Google that your page is highly beneficial and should be considered for first-page ranking.

From there, it becomes a chain reaction. As quality inbound linking increases, your PageRank increases, and with it your author and brand authority. These signals trigger your page to show up higher in search engine results pages more often, which triggers more clicks, which triggers even more visibility as Google returns personalized results based on users' search history.

Images should be created with the same strategic approach you take for generating . . . any other content.

With a clear understating of how inbound links, website authority and personalized search can inform SERP rank, you can conceptualize how creating an engaging image, such as an infographic, could potentially help your web pages rank better.

A Link Magnet Story

Back in 1996, before Google even existed, the Internet was a Wild West frontier. That's the year Bruce (now considered a founding father of search engine optimization) began pioneering how to make web pages more visible in search results.

The problem was, search engines were constantly in flux. Countless search engines emerged and either evolved, merged or faded away rapidly. To make sense of the chaos, Bruce created a chart showing the data relationships between all the different players. The image he created is recognized today as one of the Internet's first infographics (see Figure 7-4).

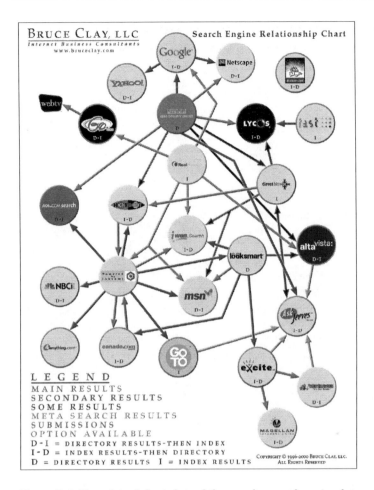

Figure 7-4: *The original chart showed the complex search engine data relationships that existed in 2000.*

Now, here's the beautiful upside of useful content. Once the Search Engine Relationship Chart® went up on Bruce's website, everyone wanted a copy. Bruce saw the opportunity and made it downloadable, and soon charts bearing his logo were hanging on company walls everywhere — in the first month alone, there were 300,000 downloads! People then wanted to follow Bruce, and because social media didn't exist yet, they went to his website. Bruce Clay, Inc. became a brand virtually overnight.

Over the years, Bruce has updated the chart repeatedly to match the changing search engine landscape; a full histogram of its metamorphosis can be viewed on the company website.[4] Today's version, which is far simpler than its predecessors, is still a downloadable file (see Figure 7-5).

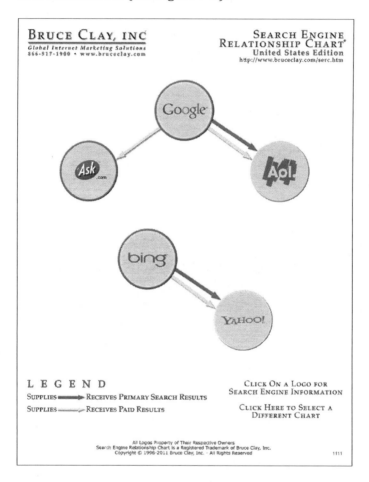

Figure 7-5: The current Search Engine Relationship Chart®

How to (Try to) Create a Viral Image

If your goal is to boost your SERP rank by creating an image that people will want to link to, it's important to *remember that viral images are content, too*. As such, images should be created with the same strategic approach you take for generating videos, blog articles and any other content.

First and foremost, make sure your image is engaging, optimized and targeted. Keep your demographic in mind; think about what interests they have, what they need and how you can best serve them. Think about their preferences for color, style and voice. Take a look at other content you and your competitors have created to see what already exists, what has been successful, what has failed and where the content gaps are. Then — perhaps most importantly — put on your creative thinking cap (or hire a designer who wears the cap better than you) and use all of the information you have collected to tell a story with your image.

How to Release a Viral Image

After you have your image created and you are ready to launch it into the world, it's important to remember three things:

- **Publish the image on a web page with value-added supporting text.** Yes, you want the image to spread, but ideally you want people linking to a text-rich page on your site rather than taking the image and posting it on their own site or social network. To encourage links to your site, it's wise to attach a benefit to visiting your actual web page. For instance, maybe you can have a large-scale PDF version of the image or infographic available for download from the web page, or maybe you include text that gives more context to the infographic, such as what inspired it or how the information in the image should be used.

  If your image goes viral, it will be shared all over the Internet in all kinds of ways that you can't control.

- **Make sharing easy.** Since you want people to share the link, it's important to make sharing easy and accessible. Consider supplying HTML embed codes that include a link back to your website built into them. This is a subtle way to improve user experience (by making it easy for users), share the love (by giving them permission to use your content on their website), and set up an inbound link that points users and search spiders back to the original source of the content (your website).

- **Brand the image with your logo and a URL.** If your image goes viral, it will be shared all over the Internet in all kinds of ways that you can't control. People are going to be tweeting the image and putting it in their blog posts without links that direct traffic back to the source. This is inevitable and impossible to control, so be proactive. Brand your images and infographics with your logo, a copyright and a backlink to the web page that houses the image. Consider also including an enticing call to action like "learn more tips" or "download the full-size image." Just remember that content is the first priority here, so the logo, copyright and link don't need to be too conspicuous. People know to look at the bottom of images for this type of documentation, so they'll be able to find it even if you keep it understated.

Closing Remarks in the Case for Image Content

We live in an attention-deficit world where content, images, videos and web pages — both good and bad — are created and published by the thousands every day. We all consume massive amounts of media, so we've constructed strong filters to allow only the most personally interesting content through. People want access to information that is engaging, helpful and available when they need it. If you have it, they'll take it. If you don't, they'll easily get it somewhere else. So, with hundreds, or sometimes thousands, of competitors saying the same thing, how can your brand get noticed in social media timelines and search engine results pages? It's time to think outside the text.

People are visual creatures. Knowing this, use images to tell your story at a brand level, as well as an individual-article level. Be thoughtful about the images you capture or create and make sure you're focusing on relevance, quality, engagement potential and demographic need. Remember, it's about the message.

Adding images to your blog and social media posts will increase engagement and optimization, but it's important to remember that real people — your customers — are looking at your images. So it's critical that your image inclusions are thoughtful and strategic. Never add an image to your article or social post haphazardly, just for the sake of adding an image.

No one wants to see the same guy with a megaphone over and over again. Choose images that will have impact and inspire shares, links and word-of-mouth marketing.

Carry your camera with you to live events, think about what you want the image to accomplish when you snap the shutter or open Photoshop, and try to include images that add something to the conversation. Aim for images that approach storytelling from angles that your competitors weren't slick, quick or creative enough to capture.

Chapter Notes

[1] "What is the maximum size for files I upload?" Facebook Desktop Help, accessed November 5, 2013. <https://www.facebook.com/help/270699543014290?sr=2&sid=0fGVW LZwegMJ2N2jn>

[2] Dan Zarella. "[Infographic] How to Get More Likes, Comments and Shares on Facebook." 2012 study. <http://danzarrella.com/infographic-how-to-get-more-likes-comments-and-shares-on-facebook.html>

[3] Jakob Nielsen and Kara Pernice, "Eyetracking Web Usability: Images." Pearson Education, Peachpit. 11 December 2009. <http://www.peachpit.com/articles/article.aspx?p=1412019&seqNum=3>

[4] "Search Engine Relationship Chart® Histogram." <http://www.bruceclay.com/serc_histogram/histogram.htm>

Chapter 8

Live Events: Where I Get to Tell the Story

You might be asking, what do live events have to do with content marketing? We'd say everything.

Events are an incredible opportunity for you to create the storyline. When you produce or sponsor an event, or commit your company to creating content around an event, you frame the conversation. You are the one telling the story. It's an influential position to be in for the perception of your own brand and for the creation of partnerships.

PR people love events, and so should content marketers. If you want to create lots of content that can be shared with and by a specific audience, then live events are your ticket. They make that kind of interactive content much easier to generate.

Why Events are a Gold Mine for Content Creation

An event can be a focal point of much of the content you create, from blog posts to videos to paid advertising, and it can offer a great story to tell. Whether your company is throwing the event, sponsoring it or, to a lesser extent, simply attending it, you'll have an array of opportunities to create content that reaches a wider audience and integrates your messaging with a new set of topics.

Murray once personally shot 70 videos and hundreds of photos during a two-day event. He spent the weeks leading up to the event talking about the fact that he'd be there, had dramatic success networking at the event because of what he was doing, and had a ton of content afterward to extend the experience and keep telling the story. This gave him hundreds of chances over two months to tell his personal brand's story. The event enabled him to align himself with other successful industry people and organizations, and even get significant exposure to their existing audiences.

One of the challenges of content marketing is content creation. How do you find the right topics to talk about in content that people will share? Events can help to solve this problem. An event by its nature brings together a lot of people. Making people part of your content naturally inspires them to share it. So an event is the perfect setting for creating shareable content.

At the same time, an event is one of the few scenarios in which you can act as content *guide*, rather than the sole creator. If you are throwing the event, you can set the schedule and create opportunities within the event that are tailored to the kind of content you want to generate. The Ford photo booth example (from Chapter 7) is a great example of this. And there are many more.

Success Stories of Event-Based Content Generation

Example 1: Red Bull

Almost every marketing activity Red Bull does works. They have done a masterful job of aligning their brand with more than just a drink, but with a high-octane lifestyle that appeals to their audience demographic — mostly men between the ages of 18 and 35. They've accomplished this feat largely through high-quality content marketing.

A recent article profiling the company's marketing observed:

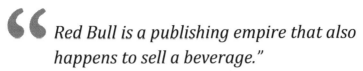 *Red Bull is a publishing empire that also happens to sell a beverage."*

– James O'Brien for *Mashable*[1]

Red Bull uses live events to create highly branded content that gets local, national and international press coverage and lots of social media sharing. The company promotes numerous events, from extreme sports competitions to modern-art shows, including many that Red Bull either organizes or sponsors in some way and promotes on its website (see Figure 8-1).

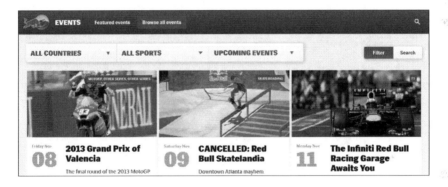

Figure 8-1: Events featured on Red Bull's website align the brand with an extreme, high-energy lifestyle.

Still, you do not have to be Red Bull to make events work for you.

Example 2: VigLink

Murray once consulted for a company named VigLink (*http://www.viglink.com*), which monetizes Internet forum communities in the online forum space. The challenge for VigLink was to reach those forum owners. During the research phase, he discovered that no event existed to connect forum community managers to each other.

So Murray helped VigLink create an event called ForumCon (*http://www.forumcon.com*) that was designed specifically for forum owners. Now in its fourth year, ForumCon is the de facto industry event for Internet forum owners. Major companies line up to release their products at ForumCon.

The conference was launched as its own separate brand. This made it an industry event that could welcome everyone, rather than just a sales pitch for VigLink. Because it met a need, it worked.

Weave into your event clever opportunities that foster a great time, market your brand, and allow your attendees to tell your brand story.

ForumCon gave VigLink a hook for lots of content marketing. One key part of the strategy was finding ways to connect the event to lots more people than just those who were attending. Here was the strategy:

1. **Distribute videos in advance:** Prior to each event, they created a video series introducing the speakers and key influencers in the sector. These people, in turn, shared the videos, with information about the event and VigLink, through their companies' social profiles and newsletters.

2. **Partner with the press**: Murray formed partnerships with key media outlets to also carry these intro videos.

3. **Have a Twitter wall:** At the event, a Twitter wall was set up that connected the whole community (see Figure 8-2). Attendees tweeted more (using the conference hashtag) because of the visibility.

4. **Post photos:** After the event, they posted photos and videos of the event. This content was also posted in media outlets and on the sites of the participating sponsors.

Figure 8-2: A Twitter wall displays what event attendees are tweeting in real-time by hashtag. (Photo credit: Twitter wall! by whatleydude, on Flickr. CC BY 2.0: http://www.flickr.com/photos/whatleydude)

How to Build Content Creation into the Flow of an Event

Events are all about travel, networking, learning more about something you love, exploring a new place, and having conversations about niche subjects with folks who can relate. They're exciting, fulfilling and social — plus, they include days on end where hundreds or thousands of people interested in what you do are walking around, glued to mobile devices that have cameras and social sharing apps.

So, as an event coordinator, how can you capitalize on social media connectedness and turn anticipation, participation and event afterglow into a gold mine of created and curated content?

The trick is to know your audience and weave into your event clever opportunities that foster a great time, market your brand and allow your attendees to tell your brand story with their own words and images.

> *Give people a memorable reason to take and share photos of themselves in a specific place that happens to have your logo plastered on everything.*

Bring together a marketing team that knows your niche market, attends a lot of events and has a knack for thinking outside the box. Your team will find countless ways, but we'll get you started with **six ideas for working content marketing into your event planning:**

1) Use the Registration Process

Set up a registration table at the entrance of your event and photograph everyone as they are arriving. With the photos, you can potentially tag all the attendees on social media and connect with all of their audiences with your logo in the background. If you name the people correctly, then your site and brand will also be found in image searches when people are looking for themselves. You can also use these photos on your blog and in marketing materials. If you are lucky, attendees will also repurpose the photos.

2) Coordinate a Niche Celebrity "Meet and Greet"

Who do your attendees look up to? Give them something to talk about by offering a few select individuals the chance to have a one-on-one Q&A session with an industry thought leader. The trick is to put out a call to action that requires a tweet response with a designated hashtag to be considered for entry.

Why it works: This activity inspires content creation before, during and after the event. The contest promotion, call to action and tweet submissions take care of pre-event user-generated content; a photo opportunity with each winner and the thought leader will make for engaging social media coverage during the event; and a long-form write-up of the Q&A sessions gives you an engaging and informative post-event blog post.

Connecting industry celebrities to your event like this is also a great way to inspire local or national press coverage, build up the perceived authority of your brand by having your event associated with the industry leader, and strengthen network connections between your conference and the celebrity.

3) Have an Industry Mascot, Artifact or Meme for a Photo Op

Sometimes a little novelty can go a long way when it's something that your audience is fanatical about. Think beyond industry thought leaders and celebrities; are there any mascots, cultural artifacts, memes or other niche novelties that your attendees can't get enough of? And is there a way you can convince the owners of these cultural novelties to allow attendees to take photos of themselves with said novelties for an allotted amount of time during your event? People like to take and share photos of themselves; your job is to give them a memorable reason to take and share photos of themselves in a specific place that happens to have your logo plastered on everything.

If you get the media on your turf, you can have a big impact on what story they end up telling.

Real-life example: For the 2013 South by Southwest (SXSW) music, film and interactive conference, the independent news company Mashable set up a branded lounge area and arranged for Internet meme sensation Grumpy Cat (and his less grumpy owner) to be available for photos during select hours. Since this was the first public appearance of Grumpy Cat, people were lined up for several blocks and some waited hours to take their picture with the cat, who was strategically placed in a Mashable-branded cat bed in front of backdrops that were covered with the Mashable logo and the #SXSW hashtag.

In this case, the content inspired was both socially curated (by people taking photos of themselves and others at the branded conference event) and also professionally created after the fact by national news sources like CNN Tech, who were drawn to report on the event[2] (see Figure 8-3).

Figure 8-3: Celebrity appearances at an event can prompt press coverage.

4) Set up a Photo Booth that Shares Branded Photos to Social Media

Can't get Grumpy Cat? Lucky for you, people still love to take photos of themselves — even without the cat! Set up a photo booth, tack up a backdrop with your brand logo on it and let people get nutty taking pictures of themselves with their new expo buddies. The trick to getting the most out of this classic is to rig your photo booth with technology that allows attendees the option to share their photos to Facebook, Instagram or Twitter right from the booth.

Real-life example: At the Facebook F8 conference, attendees received RFID (radio-frequency identification) tags that were connected to their personal Facebook accounts. With these badges, they could interact with a custom photo booth experience that let them tag themselves and publish their images to Facebook right from the booth.

5) Promote Small-Scale Interactive Challenges that Reward Participants for Posting with the Event Hashtag

People are naturally competitive, they like to win, and they're often willing to jump through some hoops for a prize. That said, you can encourage attendees to tell the story of their event experience through social media by putting together content calls to action and incentives for completing them.

Events provide content creation opportunities even when you're just an attendee.

For instance, you might ask attendees to answer a question like, *"What is the most valuable thing that you learned today?"* using the event hashtag. Then, as an incentive, choose one response to receive a free ticket to next year's event. Or, you could come up with your own event-specific clout scoring system, publicize the system along with the contest rules, and offer a tablet to the attendee with the highest score, based on their three-day social media coverage of the event.

Mini challenges like this are a great way to motivate attendees to tell their side of the story, which can help get them engaged and excited both prior to and during the event itself. Seeing content roll in from their peers can also be a great way to publicize the event. People who have never attended can get a better understanding of the size and scope of the experience and whether it would be a good fit for them personally.

6) Invite the Press

Events are a great way to get press coverage. If you can get media makers to attend, even footing the bill for them, then they are likely to cover your event and your company. They too are under pressure to produce content, so if they spend time at your event, they'll naturally gather information for their own content creation.

Real-life example: Automakers ferry auto-industry journalists and influential bloggers to locations where the journalists can get sneak peeks and test drives of the newest models.[3] The journalists do not *have to* write about the cars, but what else are they going to cover while they're there? The new cars are the only story in front of them. If you get the media on your turf, you can have a big impact on what story they end up telling.

Content PR Secrets: Optimizing an Event to Attract Media and More

By Lisa Buyer

Optimizing, socializing and publicizing an event is about enticing attendees, but it's also about attracting and engaging the people who are not attending—including the media, bloggers, and high influencers.

That concept caught my social PR eye at SES London, where Mel Carson presented a case study that showcased Microsoft Advertising's use of live tweeting, blogging, video interviews, image sharing, and other on-the-spot journalistic tactics to bring conferences to life for the people who couldn't attend.

"Your goal should be to bring the event alive for your global audience," Carson stated. The idea is to create excitement by posting content before the event starts, then, "once there, make it your goal to connect to your Internet audience with lots of blogs, tweets, and photographs."

The Microsoft Event Action Plan

In his case study, Carson described an aggressive Microsoft social PR plan that included hourly, on-the-ground tweeting and blogging, as well as a detailed film schedule of interviews with conference delegates, speakers, and their own executives.

Content PR Secrets: Optimizing an Event to Attract Media and More
(continued)

This level of planning and execution really helped to bring the event alive for the thousands of interested bloggers, advertisers, marketers, and creatives who could not make the event.

What was the result? Microsoft's branded coverage chalked up more than 40,000 interactions, or "brand engagements," including ample numbers of people reading the company blog, watching videos, browsing photos, and engaging with them on Twitter.

The Microsoft Social PR Plan Can Work for You, Too

Keeping content organized, relative, and actionable proved to be the best bet for Microsoft, and it can work for your brand, too!

Think about it: News nuggets delivered in innovative ways stick in the mind and resonate with audiences, especially:

- Live tweets
- Liveblog posts
- YouTube video interviews of speakers and industry experts at events
- Instagram reports of speakers/sessions that include key messages
- Event-specific Pinterest boards that pin relevant coverage from industry sources
- Live event images shared on Facebook, Instagram, Pinterest and Tumblr

Whether it be a conference, grand opening event, product launch, or some other gathering, there's a lot of opportunity that can be found in news-jacking your own event. Plus, strategically curating images and videos to publicize events can also create a great social PR library and historical timeline.

The trick is to start the process before the event, keep it going throughout the live experience, and then continue on after everyone's gone home.

Lisa Buyer is author of *Social PR Secrets* and was named one of the Top 40 Digital Strategists for 2013. Contact Lisa on Twitter @LisaBuyer, or visit her website at *http://thebuyergroup.com*.

Making Content as an Event Attendee

It does not have to be your own event for you to gain traction. Events provide content creation opportunities even when you're just an attendee.

If you can create great content from someone else's event, you can get huge value out of your investment to be there, beyond what you might learn. Just create more and better content than anyone else there, and you have the potential to own the conversation around the event.

Sometimes just publishing content faster than anyone else can make an impact.

Look at what kind of content was created the year before and set up a plan for what could make the content around that event better. Then execute that content yourself. Sometimes just publishing content faster than anyone else can make an impact. Professional photographers and video crews can take a week or more to get content live. If your photos and videos are up fast, the people who are writing about the event will want to use those assets. If your watermark is on the photos and videos, your brand will be part of their write-up.

How to Create Content While Attending an Event

To get the most out of live-event content, approach the event you plan to attend as you would any other content creation project:

- **Familiarize yourself with the target demographic.**
  Who is attending the conference? Who can you expect to meet there? Who would you ideally like to meet there? What are their preferences? What language and tools do they use to communicate?

- **Strategize your objectives.**
  Wrap your head around what your brand has to offer the community and decide what your objectives are. Do you want to cover the event to create blog posts that drive traffic? Do you want images with your logo to spread brand exposure? Do you want to align your brand with specific industry leaders to improve your niche authority? Do you want increased word of mouth marketing?

- **Tell a story!**
  Capitalize on all three phases of a conference: before, during and after. Use anticipation and excitement to your benefit, be in the right place at the right time during the event, and be a resource to extend the experience and keep telling the story after the event ends. As an attendee, you won't fully know what to expect, so plan to be on your toes at all times. Carry your camera with you and shoot more than you think you need to. Be a photojournalist, put your own spin on event happenings, synthesize event takeaways for those who can't be there, or create your own storyline by asking questions.

- **Plan ahead, but be flexible.**
  To help you be in the right place at the right time as much as possible, familiarize yourself with the event schedule and try to get a feel for who you can expect to be at this event. Planning the story you want to tell will help you avoid getting overwhelmed by shiny objects and packed agendas.

  Decide which of your to-do list items are flexible and which are indispensable. This bit of planning will help you minimize the number of missed opportunities if your event goal is to take home days' worth of content. That said — you really don't know what is going to happen at an event until you get there, so regardless of the schedule planning you do, don't forget to be agile. Sometimes the best plan is just to plan to be alert and flexible. Remember that first and foremost, you're a storyteller. If the story is right in front of your face and not in room B467 where you planned it to be, stay put and cover the story!

The keys to any event-based content creation is to connect with others in meaningful ways, get the most out of timing (planning for content creation not only during the event, but also before and after), and make sure your efforts tell a story and have a purpose.

Posting Event Content

When you're ready to post the content you created at a live event, here are a couple of final tips.

- **Use the event hashtag:** We've mentioned several times in this chapter how well event hashtags pull related content and people together. So you definitely want to use it in your Twitter, Facebook and other social media environments.

  If you are writing about an event, be it yours or someone else's, consider using the event hashtag in your blog post title, as well. People follow the hashtags for events they are interested in and use it in general web searches. If you put the event hashtag in your blog post title and people share your article link, then every time it is shared it will appear in the stream of conversation connected with the event.

- **Be timely:** Timeliness around events is crucial. If you are going to create content at an event, pushing some of it out while the event is taking place or immediately afterwards helps you to catch the attention of the attendees. You can then release the remaining content over time to keep the conversation going and get online leads.

Summing It Up

Whether you're the grand maestro running the event, a gold-level sponsor, or just a patron attending with an extra-large SD card in your camera, events can be like supersaturated content sponges just waiting to be squeezed.

It's all about being in the right place at the right time, facilitating conversations and creating storylines that get people thinking about your brand and the event.

If you're the event coordinator, you have the ability to guide the event experience and, accordingly, the storytelling process. Take advantage of this power to lead and funnel conversations by working into your content marketing strategy contests, meet and greets, and other on-site opportunities that will spark user-generated content and media coverage. Make sure to get brand logos in the right places, plan ahead to create photo-opportunities and experiences that get people sharing with mobile devices, capitalize on the natural flow of the event (*they have to go through registration anyway, why not take that opportunity to snap some pictures?*), and use technology to make your life easier (*think photo booth set up so that event goers can easily post images branded with your logo to social networks*). Also remember to consider content creation not only during the event, but also before and after.

> *Be flexible, be social, and keep in mind that first and foremost, you're a storyteller.*

If you're an event attendee, you'll be less focused on directing traffic and more focused on capturing moments, uncovering stories and spinning coverage to represent your brand perspective. Remember to think like a photojournalist, shoot more photos than you think you need, keep in mind the needs of your target demographic when you're deciding on content angles, take notes that help you synthesize event takeaways, and create your own storylines by asking questions.

Perhaps most importantly, remember to be flexible, be social and keep in mind that first and foremost, you're a storyteller. Sometimes the best stories are the most unexpected. That's the magic of attending *live* events, after all.

Chapter Notes

[1] James O'Brien, "How Red Bull Takes Content Marketing to the Extreme." Mashable. 19 December 2012. <http://mashable.com/2012/12/19/red-bull-content-marketing/>

[2] Brandon Griggs, "The unlikely star of SXSW: Grumpy Cat." CNN Tech. March 12, 2013. <http://www.cnn.com/2013/03/10/tech/web/grumpy-cat-sxsw/>

[3] Tim Higgins, "Is This Hell? Yes, but It's Heaven for Test-Driving Cars." Bloomberg Businessweek. 19 September 2013. <http://mobile.businessweek.com/articles/2013-09-19/gm-and-mercedes-marketers-love-to-showcase-their-new-cars-in-hell-mich>

Chapter 9

Social Media: Talking *with* People, Not at Them

Social media refers to any online network or community that allows people to interact, collaborate and otherwise socialize with one another. Social media networks come in many shapes and sizes and can be used for a variety of purposes including, but not limited to, content curation and creation, photo and video sharing, reviewing and commenting, gaming and online shopping (see Figure 9-1).

It's important to build a strong brand through what you share on your social media networks. It's also important to build the size and reach of those networks by talking to the people on those same networks.

In this chapter we're going to look at five industry-leading social networks — Facebook, Twitter, Google+, Pinterest and YouTube — to discuss why and how you should approach using social media as a primary part of your content marketing and optimization strategy.

Figure 9-1: This diagram maps the vast social media landscape, showing that there are many more channels than just Facebook and Twitter. (Image courtesy Brian Solis, www.briansolis.com, and JESS3. Source: http://www.conversationprism.com)

Why Content Marketing Strategy Needs Social Media

The landscape of social media has drastically changed in the last five years. What was once thought of as a pastime for teenagers has matured into an essential online marketing tool.

There are **four main reasons why social media should be a central part of your content marketing strategy:**

1) To Connect with Customers throughout the Buying Cycle

Having active networks can help get your messaging, personality, branding and products in front of more of the right people at the right time. To put this into perspective, think about how the online buying cycle moves from awareness to interest and so on until a purchase decision (i.e., conversion) is made. Now think of how many potential clients you've lost track of somewhere between interest and conversion.

Publishing content on social media networks helps you stay connected with your customers and potential customers through all stages of the buying cycle, and then reconnect with them over and over again as their needs change.

2) To Improve Branding and Perceived Brand Authority

Social media is a natural meeting place where people go for research and discussion. First impressions matter, and what visitors see when they arrive on your social pages will have a lasting impact on how they perceive your brand and your level of customer support. It may also affect the general satisfaction with your brand.

Having high-quality content that is published regularly, attentive engagement that shows your customer commitment, a clean design, and community numbers that reflect your presence in the industry can help set you apart from — and ahead of — the competition. The opposite can also be true; if you're not investing in your social media presence, you're not putting your best foot forward and may be giving your competitors an edge over you.

3) To Improve Brand Loyalty by Talking with Customers

There's a lot to be said about the experience of walking into a store and being able to have a one-on-one conversation with a sales rep or a fellow shopper. It's comforting knowing that you can ask whatever you want and that you'll be able to immediately get guidance, clarification, an opinion or a recommendation from a real person.

As a medium that thrives on peer-to-peer and seller-to-shopper conversation, social media has the power to bring that in-store familiarity to the online shopping experience by connecting customers directly to brand reps and other shoppers from around the globe.

The trick is to use social media as a community tool, not a broadcast tool. In other words, to talk *with* people, not just at them.

While phone and email still work great for customer support, being available to help customers in the social space that is the most comfortable or convenient for them shows that you are in touch with their needs and willing to go the extra mile to support them.

4) To Create More Brand Visibility in Search Engine Results Pages (SERPs)

Currently, Pinterest boards and Google+ content get crawled and can actually show up in SERPs when relevant. So having active and engaging content on those networks does give you more opportunities to have your brand show up in the SERPs — which means more opportunity for click-through and more opportunity for conversion.

As the Google social network, Google+ offers some additional SERP benefits to its users, including the opportunity for a rich snippet showing your Google+ author photo alongside your content in the SERPs, and the potential for searchers' personalized SERP results to include the likes and preferences of their Google+ friends. (We'll discuss this more later in this chapter.)

How to Use Social Media Effectively

With so many networks out there, you'll want to be careful to use your time investment in social media to best advantage. These tips give you a starting place:

- **Be choosy:** Strategically select social media channels to have a presence on. You don't need to be on all of them. Create a presence where your target audience congregates.

- **Do testing:** Get your message right with user testing, demographic research and analytics data.

- **Supplement with ads:** Consider amplifying your organic social media efforts with social media advertising.

- **Reflect your brand:** Use your cover photo (as well as your content) to help people get to know your brand personality/standards and get a feel for whether or not your brand is an organization they would like to buy from or align themselves with.

Social Media Is Not a Broadcast Medium

Talking *with* people rather than at them means integrating with partners, crowdsourcing and implementing interactive elements into your ongoing social media strategy. Social media is not a broadcast medium. While many people say this, even more are still treating social media as a way to simply put their content out there.

It's so much more than that. In the realm of social media, one plus one can equal far more than two.

Content marketing is best done when you can get a number of parties together to collaborate. There is a saying that "big gets bigger." The more parties you can get involved in something, the bigger it will grow.

CASE STUDY
Ford Motor Company Taking Content Seriously

 By Ric Dragon

Imagine if someone had given the US automobile industry a tarot card reading six years ago. They would probably have pulled the card showing the tumbledown tower —the one that means your whole world is being turned upside down. Indeed, there have been bailouts, loans, spin-offs, and a general decrease in sales. It's also been a time of rapid innovation and re-invention. One of the places you can witness this is in taking a close look at how the Ford Motor Company is using social media.

If you've ever experienced a presentation by Ford's global head of social media, Scott Monty, you'd probably remember his impeccable sartorial sensibility and his golden-era-radio-announcer voice. He's also been a key thinker in how a global enterprise can use social to create real value. I recently had the pleasure of catching up with Monty and hearing about Ford's latest endeavors in social media.

Being "always-on" with Content

Monty first gave me some background and big-picture information about social media at Ford. It's a global enterprise with a lot of different brands, as well as different departments at the corporate level. A big aspect of their work in social lies with communications for the corporate branding aspect, while marketing owns another part that deals with community management and having an impact on sales. On top of that, the company has a marketing agency of record as well as a social media agency of record.

Content is playing a key role. As Monty told me, "Our marketing is moving away from a campaign mentality, to an 'always-on' mentality. That requires a lot of content."

You can see some of that content if you check out the "One Tank Adventures" being created by viral video impresario Devin Graham. Ford provides Graham with a vehicle and one tank of gas. For his part, Graham, who is well known on YouTube as "Devin Super Tramp," does seemingly insane feats. The automobiles included in the videos aren't at all the main player of the story, but as Monty said, "the vehicle is literally the vehicle to help them accomplish their adventures."

Several years ago, Ford embarked on a program called the "Fiesta Movement" in which the company loaned 100 cars to 100 individuals for six months. In return, the participants were asked to create one video for each month. In refreshing the program this year, Ford reintroduced the program, partnering with different media outlets such as X Games and Bonnaroo to give it scale. In the updated program, the participants were told that all of their photos and videos would be the *sole* basis of all of the company's advertising for the model for the coming years seemingly insane feats.

Case Study – Ford Motor Company Taking Content Seriously
(continued)

Ford is demonstrating the very philosophy that has been at the heart of the whole content marketing movement. Monty declared,

"We're having to educate ourselves on the difference between advertising and content."

Because of their scale and talents in the organization, a company like Ford is able to experiment on a level that is difficult in smaller companies. Their experiments are providing us with case studies and templates for successful approaches to what is at the heart of the social media revolution: that instead of being self-promotional, there is an opportunity to create real value through excellent content.

Ric Dragon is CEO and chief strategist for DragonSearch, a leading niche player in Internet marketing. He is the author of *Dragonsearch Online Marketing Manual* and *Social Marketology*, an artist, jazz drummer, and event speaker. Connect with him on Twitter @ricdragon or his website *http://www.dragonsearchmarketing.com.* This article originally appeared on Social Media Today.[1] Reprinted by permission.

Consider Content as Social Objects

A *social object* is something that sparks conversation and sharing. So content marketing is about creating and disseminating social objects. Here's an insightful definition:

 Human beings are social animals. We like to socialize. But if think about it, there needs to be a reason for it to happen in the first place. That reason, that 'node' in the social network, is what we call the Social Object."

– Hugh McLeod[2]

Social media is made up of content generated by users. Users love to share great content, so your objective is simple, really. You need to make things that they want to share.

What Makes Content Shareable

The looming question in social media marketing is what makes something "shareable." In a word, the answer is *connection.*

When people feel a connection to a social object, they naturally use it to connect with others. A provocative photo is a great example of a shareable social object: it's easy to share and just as easy to have a conversation around. Users can have a shared experience around it, then share the photo and extend the experience. **Here are four proven ways to make your content more shareable:**

1) Involve People

While launching his blog (*http://MurrayNewlands.com*), Murray read a book called *Made to Stick*.[3] One of the stories from that book "stuck" in his mind.

The story was of a local newspaper in a small town in America. This paper was surviving the newspaper downturn and doing well. What was its secret for success? The editor said it was simple: if they could publish the names of everyone in the town in every copy, they would. The thinking was that if your name was in the paper, you would connect with it, buy it and get your friends to buy a copy, too. If you or people you know are in the paper, don't you buy it?

Figuring out ways to involve partners and people who are active in social media is critical.

Murray followed the same philosophy when starting his blog. He interviewed people he knew who were bloggers and posted the interviews on his site. The bloggers talked about the posts with their readers, often linking to the interviews and sharing them on Facebook and Twitter. This connected their audiences with Murray and earned him backlinks. Those links helped his interviews to rank well for the bloggers' names and the names of their blogs, which he was sure to use as keywords when optimizing post titles. As a result, traffic flowed to his blog through these links, and his well-ranked posts began showing up in search results for those bloggers' highly searched names — an effect that compounded over time, making his blogger interview series increasingly popular. The more popular it was, the bigger it got. It snowballed.

In any content marketing campaign, figuring out ways to involve partners and people who are active in social media is critical — in fact, it's one of the things your strategy should focus on.

As Murray's social media presence grew, so did his opportunities. In addition to more business and contacts, his growing social media presence landed him a book deal with John Wiley and Sons.

As the interviews progressed, he advanced this concept a step further. He would ask interviewees to list bloggers they admired during the interviews. That was complimentary to the people who were being mentioned, and they would usually read the posts with their names. Since they were often well-known bloggers, it meant that people with big audiences were sharing the interviews and linking to his blog.

Author Chris Brogan did something similar with his book on Google+. Targeting an extended reach, he included many examples and quotes from notable Google+ users. He knew that when the book came out, they would share being featured with their own audiences. One chapter in Brogan's book, for instance, profiles an assortment of well-known leaders who implemented Google+, from technology writer Mike Elgan to spiritual advisor Deepak Chopra.[4]

As these examples show, whether you're a small business owner, independent author or big brand, one of the best ways to get the conversation around your product moving is to make the content itself include other people you want to be involved in the sharing.

2) Use Established Content Producers

Someone recently asked Murray how to create a viral video. This was his answer: "Find someone on YouTube who has made very popular videos about a topic related to the one you're interested in, someone who could reach the audience you want to reach. Ask them to make the video, and then do everything you can to promote it — and that is how to go viral."

They laughed, but he's done it. The people who know how to make popular videos in a field are the people who are at home in that field already. They know how to produce targeted content, and they have an audience already that is likely to share it and make it popular on YouTube. They are 1000 times more likely to make a successful viral video than someone trying to do so for the first time.

The same is true with text and photos that you want to go viral. Popular content is what's getting shared — not necessarily what's best. That can be a tough pill to swallow, but it's often the case. You can make some great content that deserves to go viral, but if no one sees it, it will fall short of its potential.

3) Build on Social Proof

While any kind of partnership is going to be beneficial through social media, partnerships with established influencers are especially powerful. If you can get the influencers in your niche industry to get on your trending topic and share your content, then you can get their fans to engage and share it, too. The *social proof* (i.e., people taking their cues from observing what others are doing) that results when an influential person approves of your content plays a big role in expanding your network and influence.[5]

The same is true for social media content. If someone is searching for a subject on YouTube and all the videos have 100 views except for one with 100,000 views, that person will most likely click on and watch the one with the high view count. We are hard-wired to gravitate toward things that are already popular. Videos with lots of views get more views. Biog posts with lots of reads get more reads. Photos with lots of shares get more shares.

We are social animals in that we want to fit in and be part of what's going on. And we tend to trust what the majority has deemed best.

4) Work with Influencers

Getting influencers to be part of your content marketing campaign, either by creating their own content or promoting yours, can deliver great results. But it's not easy to ask in-demand people to talk about your product or service. Having synergy between what you are offering and their audience makes the request much easier.

In the prominent marketing book *Contagious*, author Jonah Berger dismisses the idea of working with influencers to make content spread. He says that it's the message, not the messenger, that causes something to catch on, and therefore, influencer marketing does not work.[6]

However, there are many factors that determine the success of an influencer outreach campaign. Influencer outreach is not just about getting popular people to write about or share your products on social media. It's about developing relationships with them and then getting them to use and experience your product; then they will *choose* it and tell their friends in a genuinely compelling way.

Real-life example: Popchips is one of the fastest growing snack brands in the U.S., notably ranked #5 on the Forbes list of America's Most Promising Companies for 2012, just 5 years after the company's founding.[7] Popchips' success has been largely based on influencer marketing. Lacking a budget for traditional advertising, the start-up worked instead at getting their product into as many influential hands as possible. The word-of-mouth buzz had particular impact because of who they got to do the talking.

 We focused on getting Popchips into the hands of tastemakers and influencers wherever they were, from the fashionistas at Mercedes Benz fashion week to the passengers on Virgin Airlines."[8]

– Keith Belling, co-founder of Popchips

Who's an Influencer?

By Kristi Kellogg

Social influence scores (also known as social authority scores) are a measurement of an individual or brand's reach online. **Klout**, established in 2009, and **Kred**, established in 2011, are two of the apps that that brands and individuals use to measure that reach and influence across social channels.

Influence is determined with a myriad of engagement factors, including shares, mentions, likes, retweets, number of followers and quality of followers. It's not, however, a race for followers—a high Klout or Kred score comes from quality of interaction, not quantity of interaction.

According to Klout, "Posting a thousand times and getting zero responses is not as influential as posting once and getting a thousand responses. It isn't about how much someone talks, but about how many people listen and respond" (*http://klout.com/corp/how-it-works*).

What is Klout? Fast Facts

- Pulls data from Twitter, Facebook, LinkedIn, Wikipedia, Instagram, Bing, Google+, Tumblr, Foursquare, YouTube, Blogger, WordPress, Last.fm, Yammer and Flickr

- Klout's algorithm, PeopleRank, has more than 400 signals

- A user's Klout Score falls on a 100-point scale

- Users with Klout Scores of 63 and above are in the top 5 percent of users

- More than 400 million individuals use Klout

- More than 200,000 businesses use Klout

- Score is measured using data from the past 90 days

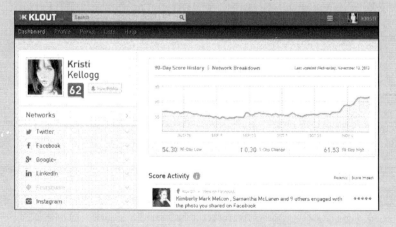

Who's an Influencer? (continued)

What is Kred? Fast Facts

- Pulls data from Twitter and Facebook

- A user's Kred influence score falls on a 1,000-point scale

- Users with Kred influence score of 600 and above are in the top 21 percent of users

- Kred also provides a separate scoring of "outreach level" (on a 10-point scale) that "reflects generosity in engaging with others and helping them spread their message," i.e., a user's retweets, replies and mentions of others.

- Users can view their Kred influence score and outreach level scores globally (Global Kred) or by interests/affiliations (Communities)

- Influence scores and outreach level scores are measured with data from the past 1,000 days

- Transparent scoring system is viewable by users

This article is excerpted from "What is Klout? What is Kred? 3 Ways to Wield Social Influence Scores for Improved Online Interactions" on the Bruce Clay, Inc. blog (*http://www.bruceclay.com/blog/2013/11/what-is-klout*).

@KristiKellogg is a content writer at Bruce Clay, Inc., journalist and social butterfly. Her articles appear in newspapers, magazines and across the Internet. Get the whole story at *www.KristiKellogg.com*.

SEO in Social Media

For the sake of keeping this section focused, we're going to stick to covering these social networks — Pinterest, Google+, Facebook and Twitter. (For YouTube tips, see "Targeting Video at Search" in Chapter 6.) Also, because social media-optimization information is always changing, this section takes a high-level approach. You — the SEO, marketing manager, social media director, etc. — must make an active effort to stay on top of the ever-changing industry. Please use this section as a jumping-off point.

What Social Signals Affect SEO?

There's been a lot of discussion about whether social media efforts contribute to search engine optimization goals. Search algorithms are frequently modified, and the way search engines do or do not take social signals into consideration fluctuates, as well. For that reason, it's challenging to try to address the topic of SEO in social media in any long-term way. The impact of social signals on search rankings is changing all the time, and Google doesn't speak up to confirm or deny the details.

Below we've listed nine social media factors and commented on them from an SEO perspective. Some of these items are currently being discussed as "potential" social signals; some of them are simply hypotheses based on observation; all of them are worth keeping in mind if you are interested in how social signals affect search engine rankings.

1) Pinterest Boards

Google crawls lots of social media channels, but it is actually very picky about what social media content it will display in search results pages. For instance, Google will not return Facebook or Twitter content; however, at this time Google does return Pinterest boards. (Note: Bing currently does not return Pinterest results, though it does include Facebook and Twitter content in its SERPs.)

For example, the email software provider Constant Contact has a Pinterest board named "Quotes for Small Business Owners" that ranks in Google for the query "business quotes." The actual pins inside the board do not rank on an individual basis, although we do see the number of total pins called out (25+ items in our example) and a couple select pins called out in an understated gray font as part of the Meta Description field (see Figure 9-2).

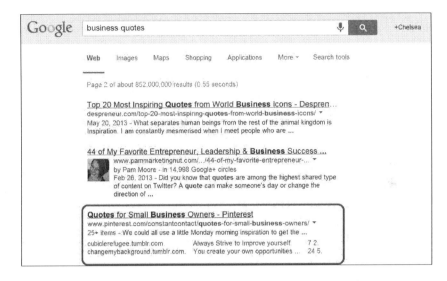

Figure 9-2: Pinterest boards can be returned in Google search results.

If you find your target market uses Pinterest, but you're on the fence about whether to adopt the social network, this ranking potential could be a tipping-point incentive.

To optimize your Pinterest boards and improve their chances of ranking, make sure to be thoughtful about the titles and descriptions you give your boards. Take care to include key phrases your target market might be using to search for content related to the theme of your board.

CASE STUDY: How Constant Contact Uses Pinterest for B2B Social Media Marketing

By Chelsea Adams

Most folks think there's no place for B2B marketing on Pinterest—the visual social media network commonly associated with wedding planning, crafting, cooking and consumer shopping. Erica Ayotte, social media marketing manager at Constant Contact, thinks otherwise.

"You can use any social media channel for B2B," said Ayotte in an early October interview she had with Social Media Examiner. "Anyone who says you can't is not being creative enough."

Having grown Constant Contact's Pinterest community to nearly 18,000 followers in the last two years, Ayotte says the trick is for B2B businesses to think outside the box and consider, at the heart of it, not what the business does but what the business is about.

For instance, Constant Contact is a software company that provides an email marketing tool. This is what the company *does*. What the company is really *about*, Ayotte told Social Media Examiner, is helping small businesses achieve their goals.

Thinking deeply about your company's larger purpose—how you intend your product to impact the end user—can make it easier to tangibly envision your target market's needs, and accordingly, to create visual, pin-worthy content that plays to those needs.

Turning Unsexy Content (Like a Press Release) into Visual Gold

If there's anything B2B marketing efforts aren't lacking, it's words. When wracking your brain to conjure up some pin-worthy visual content ideas, think about the white papers, press releases and other text-based assets you use for B2B lead generation. Are there any key statistics or quotes that can stand on their own? If so, try pulling them out and layering them on expressive stock images that support the message.

Here's an example from the Constant Contact Pinterest page:

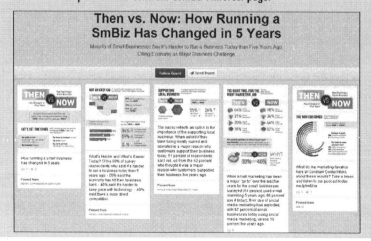

CASE STUDY: How Constant Contact Uses Pinterest for B2B Social Media Marketing (continued)

Remember to link your photos back to the original source when applicable, and to pin a mix of created and curated content to your Pinterest board.

Getting More Bang for Your Buck with Infographics

Another way to turn B2B content into Pinterest gold is to split an infographic into multiple pins. This technique helps improve user experience by making portions of the infographic larger and easier to read. It also turns one piece of content into four-plus pieces, which can help populate thin boards.

Here's an example of how Constant Contact does it:

Don't Forget that Content Curation Is Your Friend

"Part of the reason that Pinterest has grown so much for us is because we share generously and are a great curator," Ayotte told the Social Media Examiner team.

In other words, using visual quotes to link back to your own white papers is awesome, but make sure you're also linking to outside sources so your Pinterest page doesn't become a place where you spend all your time talking about yourself.

To build your following and keep your community both happy and engaged, remember to pin not with a sale in mind, but with people (and their needs) in mind. Re-pin evergreen content that represents your "what is my company really about" mission statement to build an engaged, fulfilled community of brand advocates.

Article based on *http://www.socialmediaexaminer.com/constant-contact-case-study/*

Chelsea Adams is a Bruce Clay, Inc. senior content writer interested in SEO, cob building, and energized language that motivates. Follow her on Twitter @ChelseaBeaAdams.

2) Facebook Engagement

How big is your Facebook fan base, and how engaged is your community? Google indexes the number of people who like your page, the number of people "talking about this" (i.e., people interacting with your Facebook posts by liking, sharing, commenting, checking in, tagging a photo, responding to an event, etc.) and the number of people who "were here" (i.e., people who checked in to one of your Places locations via Facebook). Then, when people search for your brand's Facebook page in Google, these numbers (with a slight indexing delay) show up in the description area of the SERPs (see Figure 9-3).

Figure 9-3: Google search results include Facebook engagement numbers (circled).

These numbers matter tangibly. They can influence how engaged your customers think you are, as well as your perceived industry authority — both of which are important factors your searchers will consider when deciding whether to endorse you, buy from your brand or just click through.

Facebook apps are the trick to capturing as much SERP real estate as you can for "Facebook [your brand]" searches.

Although Google currently reports that Facebook engagement numbers, like the number of fans a page has, aren't a factor that contributes to rankings, you should consider them an essential component that contributes to how your brand will be represented to potential customers in search results.

These engagement numbers also play a key role in determining how Google ranks your Facebook page if there are other Facebook pages with similar names — for instance, in the case of TOMS shoes, Tom's of Maine, Honest Toms Taco Shop, etc. When several Facebook pages meet the search criteria (e.g., "Facebook Toms"), Google may cluster the different brand results together, as shown in Figure 9-4 below. (Note: For details on how Bing handles this, see the section "Facebook and Bing" below.)

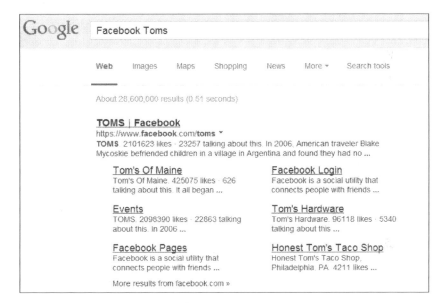

Figure 9-4: *Google clusters query-related results together, even though they may be different brands.*

When results are clustered, you want to do everything possible to be the top result. Increasing your Facebook engagement numbers (likes and people talking about your brand) boosts your chance of claiming the number one position. As Figure 9-4 shows, the TOMS shoes page had 2,101,623 likes and 23,257 people "talking about this," while Tom's of Maine had only 425,075 likes and 626 people talking; clearly, TOMS shoes' superior engagement numbers caused Google to select it for the top spot. Therefore, while community size and engagement aren't considered social signals that help your web pages rank better, they *can* impact the position of your Facebook page in search results.

3) Facebook Apps

Many people use search engines to find the Facebook pages of people and businesses. Keyword research proves it (see Figure 9-5).

Ad group ideas	Keyword ideas	
Search terms		**Avg. monthly searches** ?
nike facebook ™		880
red bull facebook ™		260
facebook nike ™		170
billy graham facebook ™		70

Figure 9-5: Research using the Google AdWords Keyword Planner shows that people often use Google to search for Facebook pages.

As mentioned in the previous section, the amount of engagement your Facebook page has can directly affect its SERP rank if there are other brands with similar names. Boosting your Facebook engagement numbers is one competitive strategy, but there's another way for you to claim the number one spot *and* several of the nested spots in the cluster, as well.

Facebook apps are the trick to capturing as much SERP real estate as you can for "Facebook [your brand]" searches.

While Google doesn't return Facebook content in the SERPs, it does crawl, index and return Facebook *apps* with a lot of engagement in clustered search results when someone searches for your Facebook page. To get more links above the fold (i.e., visible without scrolling down) for "Facebook [brand name]" queries, and to encourage more targeted click-throughs, are there any calls to action that you could turn into Facebook apps? There is a good chance an app with a lot of engagement will show up in clustered search results. Figures 9-6 and 9-7 show how one brand, Green Giant, was able to control most of the results cluster by offering apps through its Facebook brand page.

Figure 9-6: *Having Facebook apps helped Green Giant capture most of the clustered search results on Google (see circled links), allowing only 2 links to other sites.*

Figure 9-7: *The apps circled above from Green Giant's Facebook page appeared in Google's search results (shown in Figure 9-6).*

4) Facebook and Bing

Another factor to be aware of is Bing's relationship with Facebook. In early 2013, Bing and Facebook announced a collaboration that enables users to connect their Facebook profile with Bing to see search query-related Facebook content from their friends, in a column next to their Bing search results (see Figure 9-8). Bing is also powering Facebook's Graph Search feature.[9] Neither of these partnerships will help improve your SERP rank right now, but that doesn't mean it won't have an impact on how Bing results are ordered in the future. We recommend keeping tabs on how the Bing-Facebook relationship progresses.

Figure 9-8: Bing results include information from your Facebook friends.

5) Links in Twitter

The "fire hose" that once connected Twitter to Google search was disconnected in 2011. Since then, tweeted links have become 100% nofollow —they no longer pass link value, which means the links no longer help influence what Google understands to be the perceived overall relevance or authority of your web pages. While Google stopped including tweets in real-time search in 2011, it is *physically possible* for search engines to crawl Twitter links should they decide it is in their best interest to do so in the future.

6) Twitter Followers

Bing recently set up an integration with **Klout**, a company that offers a free assessment of individuals' social influence based on their aggregate online social media activity, in which Twitter activity plays a major role. (For more about Klout, see the shaded article "Who's an Influencer?" earlier in this chapter).

The Bing-Klout partnership adds Klout data to Bing search results, and people who sign up with Klout can manage their "Klout Snapshot" that displays in Bing. This Snapshot includes the user's Klout score, and some believe that individuals' Klout scores may also "push results higher or lower" in Bing.[10]

That said, while the Bing-Klout partnership *may* mean that the size of your Twitter can influence your Bing SERP representation, there is no indication that your follower count will affect Google. But, as is the case with Facebook engagement numbers, Google may decide to change its policy and consider social followers a ranking signal in the future.

7) Google +1s

Matt Cutts, the head of Google's search quality team, said in a 2013 Hacker News thread that +1s don't have a "direct effect" on Google's algorithm, and that having a lot of +1s doesn't necessarily mean that you'll rank higher.[11]

The Google +1 button is directly connected to "Search Plus Your World" — the Google initiative that delivers personal results to individuals based on their location, search history and the preferences of their Google+ friends. This means that when you +1 content in a blog or website, there's a good chance that your friends will see that content in their own search results because of your +1 endorsement. It also means that, like a chain reaction, if your friends +1 *your* content, there's a chance that friends of your friends will also see your content in their custom Google results.

Though Cutts says there is no direct effect on ranking, +1s can affect your SERP visibility (as we'll discuss shortly). And since

Google+ is owned by Google, the +1 button is definitely a social signal to monitor closely.

8) Google+ Content and Circles

How many people have you circled on Google+? It turns out that this number can impact how many people see your Google+ content on the first page of search results.

Here's how it works: not surprisingly, since Google owns Google+, Google indexes Google+ content and returns it in personalized search results. In the SERPs, the Google+ content looks just like a web page listing (see Figure 9-9).

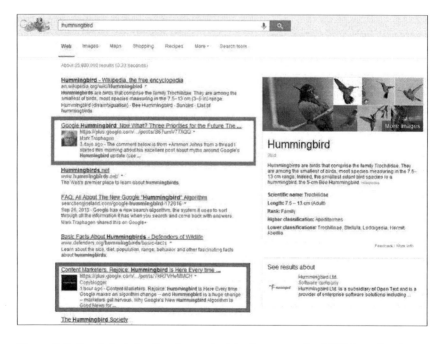

Figure 9-9: *Google includes Google+ content in the personalized SERP results of those who have the publisher circled.*

The Google+ content shows up in SERP results for three reasons:

1) Google indexes it and chooses to return it in SERP listings,

2) Google's "Search Plus Your World" algorithm returns personalized search results for every searcher based on his or her search activity and indicated preferences, and

3) The content was published by someone that the searcher
   has circled in his or her Google+ profile.

In other words, circling a person or brand on Google+ basically tells Google that you trust this person/brand, that they are relevant to your interests, and that you are interested in content from them.

People including you in their Google+ circles means they have told Google they trust you or your brand and want to receive content from you. This means more chances for Google to grab your relevant Google+ content and stick it in page one of their SERPs.

To capitalize on this, make building your Google+ community a priority. Also keep search queries in mind when writing your Google+ content. Reflect back on the keyword research discussion, and consider how people ask for things and how you can align yourself with their queries by using their own language relevantly in your content. (See Chapter 3 for more on keyword research.)

9) Google+ and Authorship

Do you have a Google+ profile, and does your Google+ profile contain your picture? The answer for any content producer should be yes. In addition, you need to include a `rel="author"` tag in the HTML of your website, blog and any articles you write so that Google pulls your Google+ profile image into the SERP results for that content (as shown in Figure 9-10).

Figure 9-10: Google search results can display the author's byline and photo (circled) from Google+.

Google Authorship: How to Do It and How It Affects SERP Rank

By Andy Crestodina

You may have noticed author faces appearing alongside some of your Google search listings. These photos are a type of "rich snippet" and appear because of Google Authorship.

Google Authorship Markup: How to get your picture in search results.

 blog.kissmetrics.com/**google-authorship**/ ▾
by Andy Crestodina - in 5,180 Google+ circles
Here are the three steps to follow to get **Google Authorship** markup working, along with tips for troubleshooting.

Because rich snippets are visually more prominent in search engine results pages, studies show they tend to have higher click-through rates—which is how Google Authorship increases traffic.

That said, unless the person who performed the search is logged in to Google+ and has you (the author) in a circle, Authorship doesn't actually affect the rank of the post. At least not yet.

Think of Authorship as a "digital signature" that verifies online profiles, puts a face to a name, and closely ties search marketing with social media. It was created to help people identify more relevant content, and—since relevance always takes precedence in search engine results pages—it tends to have a ranking advantage over content created anonymously.

How to Get Your Picture in Google Search Results

There are several ways to use Authorship to get your face to appear in Google search results, but for most marketers, the "two-link" method is easiest.

Step One: Use the "Contributor To" section to link from your Google+ profile to your content. You don't need to be active in Google+ to use Google Authorship, but you do have to set up your profile.

In Google+, fill out your basic information and upload a clear photo of your face. If you use a logo or if Google can't identify the image as a face, Authorship won't work.

On the right side of your Google+ profile's About section, there is a place to add "Contributor To" links. Add a link to your blog from there, as well as links to any blogs that you contribute to.

Contributor to
⊙ Orbit Blog (current)
🐾 Marketing Profs (current)
🔍 Social Media Examiner (current)
🌀 ProBlogger (current)
C Copyblogger (current)
🌱 Content Marketing Institute (current)
● SpinSucks.com (current)
▢ KISSmetrics (current)
🌐 Convince & Convert (current)
🔍 Social Media Examiner (current)

Google Authorship: How to Do It and How It Affects SERP Rank (continued)

Step Two: Use rel=author to link from your content to your Google+ profile. On your website or blog, use your byline or the author box at the bottom of your post to link to your Google+ profile with a rel=author tag. This tag should be added in two places: once at the beginning of the link's HTML and once at the end, like this:

Google+ HTML without tag:

```
<a href="https://plus.google.com/123">Google+</a>
```

Google+ HTML with Authorship tag:

```
<a rel="author"
href="https://plus.google.com/123?rel="author">
Google+</a>
```

So, if you wanted your bio info to say "Find Andy on Google+" your Authorship markup would look like this:

```
Find Andy on <a rel="author"
href="https://plus.google.com/123?rel="author">
Google+</a>
```

If you use WordPress, there are plugins such as Author Box Reloaded (*http://wordpress.org/plugins/author-box-2*) that will add the rel=author code for you. These plugins may also add your image and icons to all other social networks.

Why Authorship is Great for Guest Bloggers

With Authorship it doesn't matter what website the post is on, as long as the links are in place. So, if you're a guest blogger, add the host blogs to your list of Contributor To links and make sure to give the host blog a bio that includes a link to your Google+ profile with rel=author markup included. (If there's no markup added, you won't see a rich snippet; remember it's a two-link process.)

With rel=author in place and your Google+ "Contributor To" section updated, Google should make the connection and show your face within a few days. If you don't see it within a week, there is probably something wrong. When that happens, use Google's Rich Snippet Testing Tool (*http://www.google.com/webmasters/tools/richsnippets*) to check the page.

Andy Crestodina is a web strategist, co-founder of Orbit Media (*www.orbitmedia.com*), and author of *Content Chemistry: An Illustrated Handbook for Content Marketing*. Follow him on Twitter @crestodina.

Putting SEO and Social Media in the Right Perspective

Finally — social signals aside — it's important not to let thoughts about how social media affects the ranking of web search results influence you too much. Keep in mind the big picture: how social media can promote your content and, as your content changes hands virally, earn you inbound links, perceived relevance and better SERP positioning as a result.

We may not have confirmation that social activity factors into overall search engine ranking, but we do know that posting content to Twitter, Facebook, Pinterest and Google+ helps your content get in front of more people. This inarguably means more potential opportunities for quality link building, which leads to more opportunity to climb the SERPs.

Being aware of social media as a potential ranking factor can help us approach how we strategize and prioritize our social communities, but we encourage you not to overlook the forest for the trees. In other words, don't get so caught up in how social media affects your search engine rank that you forget about what's most powerful: quality content and community connection, which are primarily why we do social media in the first place.

Chapter Notes

[1] Ric Dragon, "The Big Brand Theory: Ford Motor Company Taking Content Seriously." Social Media Today, 30 September 2013. <http://socialmediatoday.com/Big-Brand-Theory/ford-motor-company-taking-content-seriously>

[2] Hugh McLeod, "Social Objects for Beginners." GapingVoid.com, 31 December 2007. <http://gapingvoid.com/2007/12/31/social-objects-for-beginners/>

[3] Chip Heath and Dan Heath, *Made to Stick: Why Some Ideas Survive and Others Die.* (New York: Random House, 2007).

[4] Chris Brogan, *Google+ for Business: How Google's Social Network Changes Everything*, Second Edition. (Que Publishing, 2013): v.

[5] Robert Cialdini, *Influence: Science and Practice*, Fifth Edition. (Boston, MA: Pearson Education, 2009).

[6] Jonah Berger, *Contagious: Why Things Catch On.* (New York: Simon & Schuster, 2013)

[7] "America's Most Promising Companies: Popchips." Forbes, February 2013. Accessed 18 November 2013. <http://www.forbes.com/companies/popchips/>

[8] Meghan Casserly, "Influencer Marketing: How Your Business Can Benefit From Popchips' Secret Recipe." Forbes, 6 February 2013. <http://www.forbes.com/sites/meghancasserly/2013/02/06/influencer-marketing-how-your-business-can-benefit-from-popchips-secret-recipe>

[9] Greg Sterling, "Bing Adds 5X More Facebook Content To Social Sidebar." Search Engine Land, 17 January 2013. <http://searchengineland.com/bing-adds-5x-more-facebook-content-to-social-sidebar-145480>

[10] Alyson Shontell, "When A Startup Worth Hundreds Of Millions Goes Dark: Klout's Quiet Year Of Growth And Struggle." Business Insider, 14 September 2013. <http://www.businessinsider.com/klout-and-startup-adolescence-2013-9>

[11] Matt Cutts, "Google +1's Correlation with Higher Search Rankings (moz.com)." Hacker News thread, 20 August 2013. <https://news.ycombinator.com/item?id=6243451>
Also reported by Matt Southern, "Matt Cutts Says Google +1's Have No Direct Impact On Search Rankings." Search Engine Journal, 21 August 2013. <http://www.searchenginejournal.com/matt-cutts-google-plus/67862/>

Chapter 10

Paid, Earned, Owned: Integrating All of My Media

Non-marketers may think that these days, there's no reason to pay for advertising. After all, you don't have to pay to open a Twitter account. Signing up for Facebook, Pinterest, YouTube and the like doesn't cost a dime. And you can make an unlimited number of tweets, posts and comments all for the same low price: nothing. With all of this "free" social media available, why would anyone need to spend money purchasing media online?

But that's uninformed thinking. Paid media *integrates* with non-paid content marketing efforts to make them more effective. It's much like squirting lighter fluid on coals: the coals might catch on their own, but a little extra fuel gets the fire going a lot faster.

In fact, marketers have classified *three* basic types of online media, all of which show the greatest results when harnessed to work together.

What are Paid, Earned and Owned Media?

The terms "paid" (or "bought"), "earned" and "owned" media

describe the different ways that media about your business gets online. Forrester Research clarified the difference a few years ago in a definitive blog post.[1] Here's a quick overview of these widely used terms:

- **Paid media** is anything that you pay to have posted. This can include advertisements, sponsorships and any kind of content that you commission.

- **Earned media** is anything that other people post about your company. This can include press coverage, fan posts on social media, re-sharing of your original content and any video or photos that other people create about your business or your campaigns.

- **Owned media** encompasses any unpaid media that you create and control yourself. This can include your own blog, website and social media accounts.

Taking a Holistic View

The lines between paid, earned and owned media are blurry today. While they used to be looked at as separate categories — something like advertisements and sponsorships in one bucket, articles written about you and word of mouth in another, and what you say about yourself in yet another bucket — the new reality is that they play off of each other.

Any content on the Internet is going to have some kind of influence on consumers. It's critical to think of all your media streams as an integrated system.

Take *experiential marketing*, for example, in which consumers become active participants in a marketing effort. Let's say you have a soft drink company and decide to set up a taste challenge for shoppers in a mall. You pay for the space and ad signage, even taking out ads in local publications. People photograph themselves and their friends sipping the drinks in front of your logo, and then post their photos and results all over their social media channels. Concurrently, you stream a live feed on your website and tweet sound bites from the tasters into your Twitter stream. Later you write a blog post analyzing your survey results and maybe even include some video snippets from the taste challenge in your next TV commercial. In this example, you've blended paid, earned and owned media together and created a unified, powerful marketing push.

Using paid media can indirectly help you achieve your SEO-related goals.

The explosion of creative approaches like experiential marketing and the proliferation of sponsored events and meet-ups all contribute to the integrated nature of content marketing. As online media, live events and the overlapping roles of PR, marketing and advertising have all evolved, the line has blurred to the point of non-existence — at least from the point of view of content marketing. Any and all content on the Internet is going to have some kind of influence on consumers. It's critical to think of all your media streams as an integrated system that can be tied back to business objectives and influence your target audience.

The new reality is that owned media plays off of or works in tandem with paid; paid and owned media can and will generate earned media; and earned media can become part of both owned and paid efforts.

Your Content Strategy: Defining Paid, Owned and Earned Media

By Michael Brito

Before getting into the specifics of a converged media content strategy, it's important to first get a better understanding of the meaning of paid, earned and owned media.

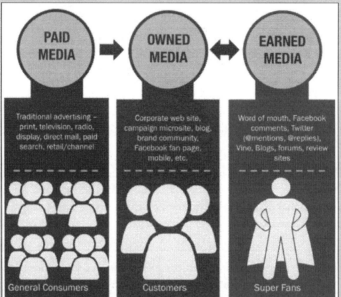

Paid media is often considered "traditional advertising" and includes banner ads, paid search marketing, sponsorships and content syndication. Paid media initiatives usually target prospects to create brand awareness or acquire new customers.

The great thing about paid media is that it scales really fast. If you have a message that you want to be seen by the mass market, paid media is the right channel to use. While it can certainly be expensive, you have complete control over the creative, content and marketing spend. The disadvantages with using paid media alone are that consumers often ignore pure "brand messages" since they are already inundated daily with advertising, and not just from your competitors either. Every large brand with a marketing message and a significant budget is fighting for their attention.

Difference between Owned and Earned Media

Owned media is the content that your brand has complete control over, such as the corporate website, blogs, communities, and email newsletters, and can extend to social media channels like Facebook, Twitter, YouTube and Instagram. Owned media initiatives typically target your brand's existing community and/or current customers.

Your Content Strategy: Defining Paid, Owned and Earned Media
(continued)

Many believe that owned media is free, particularly managing social media accounts. And while there is a sliver of truth to that, the time and labor investment is worth noting ... it takes a lot of time to create content, build a thriving community and add value to the customer conversation. You have to work with customer support teams, build escalation models, and prepare for crisis communications, as well. This takes a lot of time planning and collaborating with other team members, and time is money.

Earned media is the natural result of public/media relation's efforts, ad campaigns, events and the content you create within your owned media channels. It is not really a revolutionary concept. For several decades, brands have been hiring PR firms to reach out to the media to get them to write stories about the brand. Today, that extends to influencers who have popular blogs, as well. When someone not associated with your brand mentions you on Twitter, Facebook or another social media channel, it's earned media. Other types of earned media include consumers' social media posts, tweets, product reviews, videos, photos, and open dialogue within online communities.

Integration of Channels

While each of these channels play a critical role in your content strategy, the real power is when you can integrate two or more of the channels into one campaign or initiative. This is referred to as converged media. The same thinking has led to the recent surge in "native advertising." Sites such as Buzzfeed, Crave and Forbes are capitalizing on the opportunity to mobilize their lean but hungry editorial teams to create paid content for brands that lives alongside the site's original content.

According to the Altimeter Group, converged media utilizes two or more channels of paid, earned, and owned media. It is characterized by a consistent storyline, look, and feel. All channels work in concert, enabling brands to reach customers exactly where, how, and when they want, regardless of channel, medium or device, online or offline. With the customer journey between devices, channels, and media becoming increasingly complex, and new forms of technology only making it more so, this strategy of paid/owned/earned confluence makes marketers impervious to the disruption caused by emerging technologies.

Michael Brito is a group director at WCG, a W2O Group company. He is responsible for helping clients transform their brands into media companies by implementing social business strategic initiatives that operationalizes content strategy, scales community management and integrates paid, earned and owned media initiatives.

This article is excerpted from his book *Your Brand: The Next Media Company* (http://thenextmedia.co). Follow Michael on Twitter @Britopian.

Paid Media's Role in Content Marketing

If you create great content and want to reach the full potential for that content, paid media gives you a sure way to place that content in front of a larger target audience.

The Benefits of Pay-Per-Click Advertising

Buying ads in the search engines or elsewhere has no bearing on your rank in organic search results. Even if a company spends $100,000 a month on Google Pay-Per-Click (PPC) ads, Google's algorithm for organic search results will pay no attention.

Nevertheless, using paid media such as PPC ads can *indirectly* help you achieve your SEO-related goals of traffic, visibility on search engine results pages (SERPs) and conversions.

Here are **four distinct benefits to using paid media:**

1) Ads Work Quickly

Owned media such as your website or blog gives you the ability to put out powerful content that is engaging, helpful and worth sharing. But what if time is of the essence, and you need people to see the blog post you wrote *right now*? Paid media can jump-start the virality of owned media (and the creation of earned media) by getting your message in front of a targeted market almost immediately. This "jump-start" approach works well using search engine PPC advertising as well as social media paid advertisements and promoted posts.

2) Ads Get to Page One When Competition Is Steep

There's room for only about 10 organic links on page one of the SERPs, and competition can be tough. In some cases, local listings as well as giants like Yelp, Wikipedia and Yellow Pages take up most of the page, leaving only a few organic links for relevant businesses at the bottom (aka, where links go to die). Especially when you want to target a very competitive keyword that has a lot of page one competition, PPC advertising can do wonders to get your brand represented at the top of page one (see examples in Figures 10-1 and 10-2).

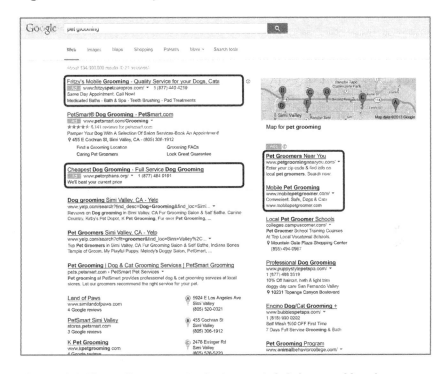

Figure 10-1: The small pet-grooming businesses circled above would not have appeared on page one at all without paid ads.

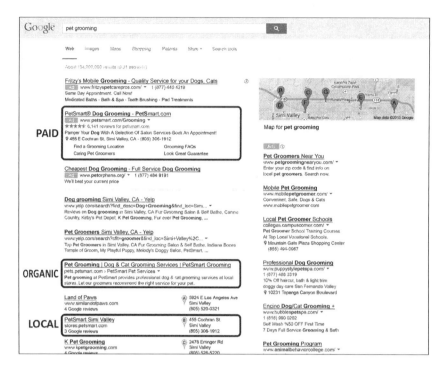

Figure 10-2: *One brand (Petsmart) appears three times in this SERP, with the paid ad showing up significantly higher than the organic or local result.*

3) Ads Give Me Control of the Message

Pay-per-click (PPC) advertising allows heightened control over the language your target market sees in the SERPs, compared to your organic search listings. With organic listings, search engines may disregard what the website owner wrote for a page's Meta Description and even Title tag, and pull whatever page text they think is most relevant to display instead. Not so with PPC. PPC advertising will always show exactly what you enter for your requested ad title and text.

PPC ads also give you more control over other elements that can draw the attention of your target market, like a displayed vanity URL, dynamic titles that can be set to include the exact search query wording, and active calls to action that allow you to collect user information directly from the ad.

4) PPC Is a Testing Lab for SEO

Being able to put ad spend behind specific keyword phrases means there's a good chance your ad *will actually show up* when real people search for those exact keyword phrases. This is important because it allows you to funnel traffic to specific keyword phrases, analyze how searchers react, and then draw conclusions about which keyword phrases resonate best with your target market.

In other words, paid search marketing gives you the opportunity to narrow and prioritize your keyword list by tracking how real-life consumers react to content in specific search scenarios. Then (*this is where it all comes together*) you can use the data you collect about the keyword preferences of your demographic to be more strategic about your organic optimization efforts, which can help inspire higher SERP ranking and increased return on investment.

How Paid Media Creates Earned Media

A key way to integrate paid and earned media is to make paid media *social*, letting it be part of the ecosystem it is advertising in.

Ideas for Turning Paid Media into Earned Media

- **Content promotion:** Sponsor your Twitter stories and promote your Facebook posts to bring them more attention. In this way, with good targeting a paid post can trigger lots of social sharing.

- **Social media sponsorship:** With social media paid sponsorship, at a live event you can specifically request people to tweet or take some action that will end up being earned. While the call to action is paid for, the action itself is done without compensation.

- **Experiential marketing:** Sampling products, hand-distributing flyers and other face-to-face marketing activities are paid ways to target live groups that will result in significant word of mouth. Paying for samples that people use and then talk about can generate great content.

- **Ads that promote campaigns:** Take out ads with a call to action that sends people to a place where they see something they can talk about or purchase.

- **White papers:** Commission white papers to be written and then give them away for free (such as in the form of downloadable ebooks).

- **Native ads:** Native ads appear amongst regular, non-ad content, and they look the same except that they're identified as "sponsored" or "suggested" for transparency. However, because people can interact with them just as they can with non-ad content (such as clicking "Like," commenting, etc.), native ads work well for many brands to seed additional content sharing.

Owned and Earned Media's Roles around Paid Media

So you've decided to take out ads or try another paid marketing effort. How can you make your owned media work alongside your paid effort to increase its influence?

How Owned Media Can Boost Paid Media

To get the most out of your advertising dollars, think about ways to amplify your message with some concurrent strategies on platforms you control. Here are some ideas for making the most of your paid media with synergistic owned and earned activities:

- **Blog concurrently:** Create blog posts, an article series or guest posts around the same themes your ads or sponsorships are focused on, and run both at the same time.

- **Bring participants to your blog:** Create ads that send potential commenters to your blog posts from an active content marketing campaign. For example, you could create an ad from your Facebook post that talks about a controversial blog post and tell people in the text that a discussion is happening there, basically encouraging comments.

- **Put ads where visitors will see them:** Run ads alongside guest posts where new eyes will find them.

- **Promote videos/photos:** Seed the sharing of paid videos/photos, either as part of a larger media campaign or as part of a follow-up to a live event, by paying a little extra to promote them.

- **Double your SERP visibility:** Run Google or Bing ads targeting the same keyword phrases that your owned media is ranking for in the search engines. The idea is to have your business represented more than once on page one, and to boost perceived authority and trust by having paid results running alongside organic results. (See the Petsmart example shown previously in Figure 10-2.)

How Owned Media Can Increase My Network and Earn Links

Want to get someone's attention? Find something *they* have written that you love and give it an earned media boost by linking to it from a blog article that you write, publish and promote. Chances are good that the big-name industry leaders that you would love a link from are monitoring their inbound links and social media mentions. So if you write a viral blog post that mentions them, they are likely to notice. And by noticing the viral post you created, they may also notice *you*.

Simply writing something that gets noticed by industry leaders doesn't guarantee that they will look at your content, much less link to it; however, it does put you in the position to be seen. Why not open a door of opportunity? Turning these opportunities into inbound links that can improve your SERP rank is all a matter of being proactive and prepared for the visibility. To get the most out of a notable leader "incidentally" stumbling upon your blog, make sure you have proactively created some stellar content worth linking to.

Earned Media and Organic SEO

Reviews as Earned Media

One type of earned media, customer reviews, can be a decision-maker for other potential customers. The best way to have great online reviews, of course, is to provide a great service that turns customers into fans. Paying for positive reviews would be unethical, but there are ways you can encourage people to write them online.

First, make sure that members of the press who like your brand get pre-release information about your products. This can stimulate positive, earned coverage of your products and services that can, in turn, influence consumer perception and drive sales.

Secondly, ask your fans if they would recommend you to other people — this will encourage them to write positive reviews. If you have lots of positive reviews, then the occasional negative review will not hurt your business much. In fact, if you only have reviews that talk about how amazing you are, prospective customers may be skeptical. Customer reviews on your website, your Google+ Local listing, and external consumer feedback websites like Yelp and Bizrate should be considered an important earned media priority.

Ideas for Maintaining Positive Reviews Online

Here are several places where press coverage and customer reviews tend to have a big impact, with our suggestions to help you capitalize on the positive, combat the negative and maintain control of your brand's reputation online.

- **In Google searches:** Research negative searches for your brand to see what's out there. Search queries to find negative information such as "[product name] scam," "[product name] sucks," and "[product name] competitor" are popular.

Many companies work hard to control how they are represented in searches like this. In his SEO training courses, Bruce suggests that companies use an offensive strategy to combat negative search results: create content around these types of queries but make it positive. For example, *"Is product XYZ a scam?"* or *"XYZ brand thinks it sucks that..."*

- **Ripoff report:** This popular site (*http://www.ripoffreport.com*) that ranks very well in Google lets consumers post complaints, but also lets brands rebut and publicly resolve issues. Many complaints on the site have been quickly and positively resolved with very happy customer reviews.

- **Your website:** Don't hide good reviews in a back corner of your website. Create a page for positive comments and reviews and link to it within your site. This helps those positive comments and reviews rank well in search engines. The engines should see your site as the authority resource on content about your brand and your products, and that authoritative site linking to the positive review helps the review rank well. (Note: Later we'll explain how to show these reviews as star ratings in your SERP listings.)

- **Bloggers:** If you have good authority for your site, bloggers seeking quality backlinks may be encouraged to write nice things about you. You can also share their positive reviews on social media. This will help them rank, encourages people to say nice things about you and gives you great content for your social media platform.

- **Yelp:** You may have noticed shops putting up signs asking customers to *"Check us out on Yelp."* While you are not supposed to ask customers to write Yelp reviews about your business, you can just encourage them to read your Yelp profile.[2] In this way you are pointing fans to your Yelp page, where they can then write reviews.

The SEO Benefits of Earned and Owned Media

Earned media (i.e., what other people post about your brand online) tends to include links that point back to your content. This represents a great opportunity to earn quality inbound links that send search engines "votes of confidence" in your content. Links from sites relevant to your business or topic can improve the perceived authority of your pages.

With content curation on the rise, the opportunity for earned media — and earned inbound "link juice" that affects your relevance, authority and SERP rank — is significant. The trick is to create user-focused owned content that adds to the conversation, helps your target audience (by informing, entertaining or other) and is worth referencing.

How to Add Reviews to My Organic Search Listings

When someone performs a search and your web page shows up, Google tells a bite-size version of your story — potentially including everything from who you are and what you do, to how much your customers value you.

Yes, Google can show single and aggregated reviews that convey customer approval (or disapproval) right in organic SERP listings. This is one type of *rich snippet* that Google displays based on special markup webmasters include in their HTML. In action, listings that include review and ratings rich snippets look like the examples in Figure 10-3:

Figure 10-3: Ratings and reviews (a type of rich snippet) can display under business listings in Google.

If you're not sure why you would want to add rich snippets for reviews and ratings to your SERP listings, we recommend looking at the images above again. Those stars pop out, a splash of eye-catching color (in actual SERPs) that can go a long way to helping your listing stand out from the pack, get noticed and stimulate click-throughs.

Reviews also convey authority and critical information to searchers trying to make a conversion decision. Just think which route you would choose if presented with two equally relevant options: one brand that has 1,067 five-star reviews and another with 0 reviews.

So, how can you take advantage of this great feature? There are **three primary steps to getting review and rating rich snippets to show up in your organic SERP results:**

1) Have a single web page on your site that is about a specific product or service (not a collection of products or services) and not "adult" in nature.

2) Make a way for customers to leave reviews for your product or service on this web page.

3) Use semantic markup to explain to Google that you have reviews on your page, what type of reviews they are (single or aggregate) and how they should be represented (e.g., 1-5 star rating, 0-100%, etc.).

TIP: *For more information, see the Google Webmaster Tools Help page on how to implement review and rating rich snippets (https://support.google.com/webmasters/answer/146645 ?hl=en).*

The Bottom Line: Think Integration

We hope you walk away from this chapter knowing at least these four things:

- It's important to think of paid, earned and owned media as an integrated system centered around influencing your target audience and accomplishing your business objectives — not as three separate bins.

- There should always be strategies that drive what you write, when you back a campaign with money, and how you manage, solicit and monitor what others write about you.

- While you can't always control what other people write about you, it's still a good idea to actively monitor and encourage positive press while proactively working to remedy the, say, *less unenthusiastic* coverage you get.

- At the end of the day, it's all about getting your content in front of more eyes, networking, putting your best foot forward, being hands-on with earned media rather than letting it run rampant (or not run at all), and doing good work that builds trust and gets people talking.

Chapter Notes

[1] Sean Corcoran, "Defining Earned, Owned and Paid Media." Forrester Research Blog, 16 December 2009.
<http://blogs.forrester.com/interactive_marketing/2009/12/defining-earned-owned-and-paid-media.html>

[2] "Don't Ask for Reviews." Yelp for Business Owners Support Center. Accessed 19 November 2013.
<https://biz.yelp.com/support/review_solicitation>

Final Thoughts

Algorithms change. Social networks change. The needs and wants of your target market change. Even the way the industry uses the term "content marketing" is bound to change.

In fact, by the time you read these words, the world of online marketing will have changed. We know this because the tactics, trends and technology that drive online marketing are *always* evolving.

We also know there are some things that never change.

Like the power of a picture that speaks a thousand words. The value of talking *with* people rather than at them. And the impact a single sentence can have when it perfectly represents your brand and perfectly embodies the essence of your target market.

We have been in the online marketing industry for years and have both experienced how shifting external factors can affect online marketing strategies. That is why we wrote this book with technology, change and the tactics that transcend both in mind.

This book — like content marketing itself — is about more than just jumping in with both feet and *doing*. It's about thinking before you jump, and considering the *why* behind what you do.

It's about taking a big-picture approach; self-reflection; goal setting; getting to know the people you're talking to; learning the nuances between engaging content and blast marketing; being proactive rather than reactive; and understanding that before your content can make an impression, it has to be discovered.

It's the difference between being a publisher who writes "stuff" and being a *content marketer* who communicates with impact.

When you commit to using content marketing and SEO to connect with your target market and generate sales, a set-it-and-forget-it approach just won't work. We recommend that you internalize the core lessons we've provided, use these pages to get your content marketing strategy moving in the right direction, and then take an eyes-open, agile approach from there. Because our industry will always be changing, please consider this book a stimulus and jumping-off point for your continued education.

Now it's your turn to tell your story. Go create something that matters.

Glossary

A

above the fold On a web page, "above the fold" refers to content that is visible to the user without scrolling down.

algorithm A set of rules a search engine uses to determine the web pages it will return in response to a query, and the order it will return them in. There are 200+ confidential factors that contribute to search algorithms, and search engines guard those algorithmic factors closely.

ALT attribute Short for "alternative text," an ALT attribute is a line of HTML code that describes an image in plain text. ALT attributes display on-screen when an image can't be rendered. They are also used to describe images to search engines and screen readers that aid the visually impaired.

analytics A collection of data that can be analyzed to track how people are interacting with a website, email, or other online experience.

anchor text The words that make up the clickable portion of a link. For instance, the anchor text in the following example is "SEO best practices": *In his article about SEO best practices, John says . . .*

authorship A Google tool that connects an individual's Google+ profile to his or her content on the web. Authorship is implemented using a small string of HTML code (`rel=author`), and, when done correctly, shows an author's Google+ photo and his or her Google+

community stats in the rich snippet for his or her article. *See also: rich snippet; rel=author*

authority   In the context of search engine optimization, authority is a word used to describe people and websites that are widely trusted and extremely relevant leaders within niche industries. The exact factors that search engines use to calculate the authority of people and web pages are proprietary and publicly unknown.

B

blog   A collection of web pages in which an individual or a business regularly contributes content. Blogs usually contain text content, but can also include videos, images, slideshows, and other forms of rich-media content.

blogging   The act of writing in a blog. Writing in or contributing to someone else's blog is often called guest blogging. *See also: blog*

bounce rate   An analytics metric that describes the number of people who enter a website and quickly leave without interacting with the entry web page or clicking to advance to another page on the site. *See also: analytics*

buying cycle   A multi-step process that describes a consumer's path to purchase. There are several buying cycle models, but generally the five agreed upon stages are: awareness, consideration, interest, research and purchase.

C

click-through rate   Often abbreviated as CTR, click-through rate refers to the number of times a link is clicked, either in search results or in other marketing initiatives like email marketing.

content audit   The act of surveying and inventorying current and previously published content to better understand whether your content strategy, in whole or in part, is effectively helping you meet your business goals.

curating content   The act of finding, gathering and publishing a collection of relevant content from internal or external sources.

E

embed code A segment of pre-written code that, when pasted into the HTML of a website or blog, adds an image, video or other interactive feature to the web page.

evergreen content A type of content that is always relevant and accurate regardless of how old it is.

G

Google "Search Plus Your World" The Google initiative that delivers personal results to individuals based on their location, search history and Google+ circles.

guest blogging *See blogging*

H

hashtag A word preceded by a pound sign (#). Hashtags are used as a search and organization tool on social networks such as Twitter, Facebook, Instagram, and Google+. Using hashtags allows network users to search for content by topic (for instance #SocialMedia).

I

iFrame An element used in web design, iFrame is short for inline frame and describes an HTML document that is embedded inside of another HTML document.

inbound link Any link from an external web page that points to one of your web pages.

indexing When a search engine spider crawls a web page it essentially takes a giant scan of the page and caches (i.e., stores) the scan as reference material in a catalog called a search index. Accordingly, this crawling process is sometimes referred to as indexing. *See also: search engine spider*

infographic An image that conveys information in an engaging, visually appealing way.

J

JavaScript A scripting language. It is often used on a website as client-side JavaScript, or to enable scripting access to objects in other applications.

K

keywords Words that people enter into search engines to seek information. *See also: long-tail keywords*

keyword research The act of using keyword research tools, like the Google AdWords Keyword Planner, to discover the exact phrases people enter as search queries.

keyword stuffing The act of adding an inordinate number of keyword terms into the HTML or content of a web page.

L

link building A search engine optimization tactic aimed at increasing the number of external links that point back to a website. *See also: search engine optimization*

link magnet A category of high-quality content that appeals to a target market and, as such, naturally attracts attention and inspires websites to link to it.

liveblog A blog post, or series of blog posts, that cover an event as it is happening.

long-tail keywords Keywords are words that people enter into search engines to seek information. Long-tail keywords are keyword phrases that contain three or more words.

M

meme As it pertains to online marketing, a meme is an image, video, or physical act that is passed on, replicated, or discussed in such volume that it becomes a viral cultural element. *See also: viral*

Meta tags HTML tags that communicate information about a web page to search engines and, when rendered in search engine results pages, to humans. For SEO purposes, the Meta tags with the highest optimization value are the Title and Description tag.

N

nofollow An HTML attribute that amends links and tells Google the author does not want this link to pass

O

OpenGraph tags HTML coding that website owners can use to allow for interaction with Facebook directly on their site. Such actions include specifying the text and image that is shared on Facebook when a site visitor clicks the "like" or "share" button on a web page.

optimize A word used to describe the process by which technical, developmental, and on-page search engine optimization tactics are applied to a website. One optimizes a website to improve their rank in the organic listings of a search engine results pages. *See also: organic search results*

organic search results Listings on search engine results pages that are not paid for, and for which search engines do not sell space.

P

PageRank A link analysis algorithm used by Google to help determine the relative importance of a website. PageRank is only part of Google's search algorithm.

personas As the term pertains to online marketing, personas are collections of consumer biographies that are created based on conversations had with actual buyers, as well as market research and analytics data. Personas help marketers pinpoint the needs and wants of their target markets. *See also: analytics*

PPC An acronym short for "pay per click," PPC refers to a form of paid advertising offered by search engines. They are called pay-per-click ads because advertisers bid varying amounts of money to correlate their ads with specific search queries, and advertisers only pay when a searcher actually clicks on the ad.

R

rank, ranking   In the context of search engine optimization, rank and ranking refer to the position of a website's web pages in the organic — or non-paid — search results. For instance, your rank is number one if you are the first organic link listed for a search query.

rel=author   An important HTML component of Google authorship. *See also: authorship*

RFID tags   Short for "radio-frequency identification," RFID tags use radio frequencies to wirelessly transfer data from one source to another. An example would be an RFID tag-rich conference badge that, using information from attendees' registration, would allow attendees to wirelessly publish photos to Facebook using only the badge.

rich snippets   Google uses the word snippets to describe additional text that accompanies links in search result listings. Snippets are transformed into more detailed rich snippets when web developers add semantic markup that tells Google more specific details about the contents of web pages. There are seven types of content that Google supports rich snippets for as of October 2013: reviews and ratings; people; products; businesses and organizations; recipes; events; and music. *See also: semantic markup*

RSS feed   Short for "rich site summary" or "really simple syndication," an RSS feed is an XML web feed that publishes frequently updated content on several specifically assigned external sites.

S

sales funnel   A marketing term used to describe the nature of the customer's path from awareness to purchase. A funnel metaphor is used because, like a funnel is wide to allow a lot in at the top and narrow to let only a little out the bottom, the sales funnel, too, sees a lot flow in at the beginning of the buying cycle, but only a small amount flow out at the end. *See also: buying cycle*

search engine optimization   The process of editing a website's content and code in order to improve visibility within one or more search engines.

Search Engine Relationship Chart® An infographic that shows the relationship between currently active search engines. The Search Engine Relationship Chart® was originally created in the year 2000 by Bruce Clay, Inc., and is updated periodically as the search landscape changes.

search engine spider The part of the search engine that reads, or "crawls," web content is called a spider. When the spider crawls web pages it essentially takes a giant scan of each page it reviews and caches (i.e., stores) these scans as reference material in a huge catalog called a search index. It's this index that Google refers to when determining in milliseconds whether your content is a relevant result that should be returned in response to a search query. *See also: indexing*

semantic markup A markup language used to help search engines more fully understand the content of web pages. Google may use semantic markup to deliver rich snippets in its search results. *See also: rich snippet*

SEO The acronym for "search engine optimization." *See also: search engine optimization*

SERP The acronym for "search engine results page."

siloing A site architecture technique used to improve search engine optimization and user experience by focusing a site through multiple themes. *See also: search engine optimization*

social media marketing (SMM) Marketing strategies that utilize social networks such as Facebook, Twitter, YouTube, Pinterest, and hundreds more. *See also: social network.*

social network An online network that lets individuals and businesses communicate with one another through posts, comments, and other forms of community-oriented content exchange.

social object Any piece of content that sparks conversation and sharing.

spam Any search marketing method that a search engine deems to be deceptive or otherwise detrimental to its efforts to deliver relevant, quality search results.

U

user experience A phrase used to describe the experience a user has when interacting with a product such as a website or a social network. Often abbreviated simply as UX.

V

video Sitemap A Sitemap is a list of web pages that helps human users and search engines understand the content and organization of a website. A video Sitemap is a specific type of Sitemap created to help search engines find and understand video content.

viral Often used in the context of content "going viral." When content goes viral it means the content was (or is being) shared thousands, or even millions, of times.

W

Webmaster Tools A toolset provided by Google or Bing that helps website owners better understand how the respective search engine is seeing their website, and whether the search engine detects any penalties or other problems that may be affecting a website's rank. "Webmaster Tools" is often prefaced by a search engine name to distinguish between the two platforms. *See also: rank*

Index

Note to the reader: Throughout this index, **bold type** indicates contributors to this book. *Italicized type* indicates illustrations or images.

Made in the USA
San Bernardino, CA
27 August 2015